WHAT YOUR
SON ISN'T
TELLING YOU

WHAT YOUR SON ISN'T TELLING YOU

Unlocking the Secret World of Teen Boys

MICHAEL ROSS AND
SUSIE SHELLENBERGER

BETHANYHOUSE

a division of Baker Publishing Group
Minneapolis, Minnesota

© 2010 by Michael Ross and Susie Shellenberger

Published by Bethany House Publishers
11400 Hampshire Avenue South
Bloomington, Minnesota 55438
www.bethanyhouse.com

Bethany House Publishers is a division of
Baker Publishing Group, Grand Rapids, Michigan

Printed in the United States of America

ISBN: 978-0-7642-1840-8

Unless otherwise identified, Scripture quotations are from the Holy Bible,
New International Version®. NIV®. Copyright © 1973, 1978, 1984, 2011
by Biblica, Inc.™ Used by permission of Zondervan. All rights reserved
worldwide. www.zondervan.com

Scripture quotations identified TLB are from *The Living Bible*, copyright
© 1971. Used by permission of Tyndale House Publishers, Inc., Wheaton,
Illinois 60189. All rights reserved.

Cover design by Greg Jackson, Thinkpen Design, Inc.

Authors are represented by WordServe Literary Group.

17   18   19   20   21   22   23   7   6   5   4   3   2   1

To my family,
Tiffany and Christopher,
I love you both
—Michael

Contents

Introduction

Mysteries of the Guy Zone

Imagine if your teenage son freely opened up and shared what's really going on inside his head. You'd probably lose consciousness, right?

And if he came home from school speaking in complete sentences—as opposed to his usual grunt-like expressions ("Uh-huh," "Naaaa," "I dunno!")—you'd be making a frantic 9-1-1 call: "Hello, police? I'd like to report an impostor on the premises. He says he's my son, but I know better!"

In reality, that once-affectionate kid who used to talk your ear off is now beginning to pull away. He's being replaced by a man-sized teen who claims your hugs "invade his space." Ironic, isn't it? Just when your son needs you the most, he shuts down. This leaves parents everywhere desperate for answers:

- I try to carry on a simple conversation, and it becomes an argument.
- I make an effort to give my advice, and it doesn't get through.
- I reach out with respect, and all I get is attitude.

Sound familiar? If you're beginning to lose patience, *don't lose heart.* During our more than fifty combined years of experience with teenagers, we've observed that just beneath a boy's alien exterior is an amazing young man who has a head full of hopes, dreams, fears, and questions, as well as a whole bunch of other serious thoughts. With a little prompting, he's very capable of sharing them—especially with Mom and Dad. And regardless of how hard it feels at times, we urge you to try.

You are the greatest influence in your son's life, and even though he doesn't always show it, your support means everything to him. That's why we're convinced that you can spark meaningful communication—more than just "Uh-huh" and "I dunno"—and nurture a closer relationship.

How? Get connected with three basic relational links—keys that can unlock the door to your son's world.

"Please Clue In: I'm Not You!"

The first relational link is *empathy.* Through the years, we've received thousands of emails from teenagers, and we've talked to young people from all walks of life and from nearly every corner of the world. The boys we meet often echo the same message to parents: "Don't tell me how it was for you. Clue in to how it is for *me*—here and now. Take an interest in how *my* world looks and feels . . . and try to understand what *I'm* going through."

This book can help. Within these pages you'll hear the voices of real teen guys, and you'll get a rare look at their secret world: an often brutal landscape that's characterized by loneliness and peer fear; one in which measuring up as a man means conforming to the Cruel Cool Code of always being a tough guy, never showing weakness, and never expressing true feelings.

You'll read what boys think and feel—and what they need from you—as they navigate a variety of challenges: confronting bullies; finding their "true identities"; battling lust and pornography; abstaining from sex; questioning homosexuality; and steering clear of drugs, drinking, and the social scene.

"Trust Me, and I'll Trust You."

The second relational link is *trust*. "I need this from my parents more than anything else," one boy told us. "I can't handle it when they think I'm doing drugs or getting into trouble, when in reality I'm not. I need them to trust that I'm a good kid—even if I stumble."

Now listen to the ache of another boy who is struggling to respect his parents: "Trust was shattered in our home long ago. Mom and Dad say stuff like, 'Don't drink, smoke, lie, fight, or cheat,' yet they do it all the time. How can I listen to people who don't walk their talk—even if they are my parents?"

Trust is fragile and is sometimes hard to build, yet it's universally important to every teen guy. It's also a primary reason the young man in your life may shut you down while other adults—such as coaches, youth ministers, teachers—can command his full attention.

We'll guide you through the issue of trust and show you why it is important to build it by earning the right to be heard.

"Stay Close and Let Me Breathe."

No doubt there's a "war of independence" going on with your son—that constant, tension-filled struggle you experience as your teen boy moves toward adulthood.

"It hurts when Mom and Dad don't have time for me," a young man told us. "But it's just as frustrating when they smother me. Give me some breathing room. Let me try stuff on my own, and even allow me to fail. I'll survive. I might even come out stronger than before."

The third relational link: consistent, balanced *connections.* This means setting parameters . . . and knowing when to step back. It means picking your battles and letting go from time to time. Above all, it means taking an interest in your son's world *every day,* and letting him step into yours.

"I want a deeper connection with my parents," says another teen boy. "I need to hear from them, 'I love you,' 'I'm proud of you,' 'I won't give up on you.' I need them to be there for me."

Face it: Teen guys are stressed out. Far too many feel the constant pressure to prove themselves in classrooms, on playing fields, and especially among their friends. Now more than ever they need change. Whether or not they're willing to admit it, deep inside they hunger for family support and connection—and they long to be accepted by their peers.

They're counting on you to teach, protect, and look after their well-being in this very big, frightening world.

These are the things your son isn't telling you. . . .

CHAPTER 1

How a Boy's World Looks and Feels

Jeanna Smith wasn't about to give up on her teenage son, Nick.

Despite a big fight they'd had earlier—and some hurtful things he'd said—Nick was a good kid. Jeanna knew he was going through some hard times right now: He was rejected by a girl he liked, he was being picked on by some guys at school, and he hadn't made the basketball team.

"Honey, you haven't touched your spaghetti," she said to her son during dinner. "You've got to eat—otherwise you'll get sick."

Nick shot a hurt look at Jeanna. "Too late, Mother," the sixteen-year-old snapped. "I'm already sick—*sick* of all the crud I deal with every day. Totally SICK of my life!"

"Then you don't have to eat," Jeanna said. "Let's talk. I'll listen. Tell me what's going on inside—"

"Where's Dad?" Nick asked.

"He's working late—"

"Again!" Nick snapped, interrupting Jeanna. "He's never around. It's just you and me. We're not a *real* family. Everything is so messed up. I just can't take it anymore."

Before Jeanna could utter another word, Nick stood up and threw his fork on the table. "Look, I don't want to talk—to anyone." With that he stormed out of the kitchen.

Jeanna slumped back in her chair and pushed her food away. Lately it seemed as if Nick was on an emotional roller coaster. He was even pulling away from Jeanna's attempts to reach out. The weary mom was scared, confused, and desperate. Most of all, she was starting to lose her patience.

As she sat at the kitchen table, she began to think about a promise she had read earlier in the Bible:

> Fear not, for I have redeemed you; I have summoned you by name; you are mine. When you pass through the waters, I will be with you; and when you pass through the rivers, they will not sweep over you. When you walk through the fire, you will not be burned; the flames will not set you ablaze. For I am the Lord, your God, the Holy One of Israel, your Savior. (Isaiah 43:1b–3a)

Jeanna rubbed her eyes and took a deep breath. *I'm barely treading water, yet I know I've got to trust. I realize I have to stay strong and not let this get the best of me.*

Later that evening, Jeanna stood quietly by her son's room and poured out her heart in prayer: *Lord, I know Nick doesn't mean to act this way. And I know that I need to be a source of strength—and reach out now more than ever. Please be my source of strength. Give me the right words and actions. Most of all, don't let me lose him.*

Jeanna tapped on the door. "Nick, can I come in?"

"Whatever."

Jeanna pushed open the door. "I just wanted to say goodnight . . . and maybe get a hug."

Nick just blinked.

Jeanna sat down on the edge of the bed and embraced her son.

Postcards From the Edge

Here's some good news for weary moms: You can improve communication with your son, guide him through all those jumbled emotions inside, and even nurture better parent/teen connections on the home front. How? You *and your husband* must clue in to the unique, boy-specific ways in which teen guys think and feel . . . and take an interest in how their world looks.

Here's a snapshot:

- He must survive a climate that in one moment is playful and childlike, then suddenly changes to harsh, overwhelming, and cruel.
- Popularity is measured by how well he does with the opposite sex.
- Rejection is a fate worse than death.
- His drive for independence is as strong as his drive for food.

- He is fascinated by those strange creatures known as "the opposite sex."
- He can't even control his own emotions from minute to minute.

You're probably thinking, *Hey, this describes my teenage years!* (Some things never change.) But while there are core issues common to every generation, boys are coming of age in a high-tech world that's vastly different from the one you and I had to navigate. His world is more connected and much more complex.

Computer technology has exploded, making it much easier for guys to interface with others anywhere in the world. What's more, families have taken a beating. Divorce rates are at record levels, even among Christian households. And in this day and age of high-tech toys and low-tech values, sin is packaged, downloaded, and made accessible to the masses as never before.

With this in mind, let's examine some key issues facing boys at each stage of development, along with ideas on how you can steer him through the challenges of adolescence.

TWEEN (Ages 10–13): Prepare for the Journey

I love music and sports and have plastered the walls of my room with all the people I love. My mom thinks I'm obsessing . . . but I think it's cool!—Tanner, 12

Girls call and text me all the time. I love it, but my parents are kinda freaking out. They've given me "the talk" again, which totally grosses me out.—Chad, 12

I admit I'm sort of addicted to video games. I think they're awesome. Mom and Dad, on the other hand, seem worried and always
lecture me about going outside and getting exercise and stuff.—
Jonathan, 11

Sometime on or before his thirteenth birthday, the average
male transforms from an enthusiastic, wide-eyed elementary
kid to an emotionally unpredictable, uncommunicative alien—
otherwise known as a teenager. One word best describes his
life during this phase of life: *change.*

Pastor and youth expert Gary Hunt says, "Regardless of
whether or not physical puberty has arrived, the middle school
mentality has led them from childhood to adolescence, from
an end to a beginning. As adolescence is the bridge between
childhood and adulthood, so the middle-school years are the
bridge between childhood and adolescence."[1]

Parents of "tweenage" boys must prepare their sons for the
journey ahead. Here are three key things you should do before
puberty hits:

Alleviate his fears. Tell him this: "Sometime soon your hormones will kick into gear, and you'll begin the transformation
from boy to man."

Explain that his growth into manhood is hereditary. He'll develop at a similar rate as his father. So Dad may want to sit
down with his son and answer a few questions: how old he was
when he began to grow taller, how old he was when puberty
hit, how he handled all the "scary" body changes.

Constantly remind him of God's plan. Despite all the different
body shapes and sizes he sees at school or in the locker room,
he can rest assured that he's normal! He is created by the one

and only God Almighty, the God of the universe, and He never makes mistakes. His timing is perfect.

Five Tweenage Extremes to Note

- Extreme hero worship
- Extreme avoidance of parents
- Extreme crushes
- Extreme humor
- Extreme energy

EARLY TEEN (Ages 13–15): The Incredible Morphing Kid

> I don't have any hair down there. In fact, my face and body still look like those of an elementary school kid, not a young man. Am I okay?—Jonah, 15

> I get erections all the time—usually at the wrong times, like when a girl walks up to me and says, "Hi!" It's totally embarrassing. I feel like some kind of sex freak.—Andre, 14

> I hate my body. Other guys my age have muscles and stuff. I'm way too skinny and short—and I have a face full of zits. Life stinks!—Braden, 15

Time magazine reporter Nancy Gibbs described the early teen years as "the age of childhood leaning forward and adulthood holding back, when the world gets suddenly closer, the colors more vivid, the rules subject to never ending argument."[2]

Boys this age have bodies that are chemical laboratories, exploding with all kinds of new activity. And with all these changes going on inside (and outside), your early teen can't help asking himself, *Is this normal? Am I normal?*

Maybe he has sprouted three inches above everyone else his age. Or maybe his peers did the growing, and he feels abnormal. It's important that you continue to alleviate his fears, assuring him that his development is a normal part of growing up.

Tell him this: "Your body is changing and you're getting a new look. Occasionally you'll wish you could hide behind a sign that says 'Stay Away—Under Construction!' But try to be patient, because when the manhood-morphing process is over, you're going to like the new you."

Your son will also probably change some part of his identity. "He will shuck off the identity you have given him as easily as he discards the clothes you buy him," Gary Hunt points out. "Some of these passing phases will be incorporated into the person he will ultimately become; others will fade away."[3]

During the early teen years, it's essential that you help your boy make sense of another change in his life—his *sexual awakening.* By now he has probably noticed a strong appetite for sex. Sadly, though, much of what he'll learn about this wondrous part of his life will come from his peers, including misinformation about girls. What's more, your teenager is being bombarded almost constantly with sexual messages from the media. Parents must set the record straight and communicate the truth about sex.

"Sexual energy," notes author Bill Beausay in his book *Teenage Boys,* "especially in someone as hormonally charged as your teenage son, is a wildly strong and surprising force. It begins in your son's life during these years, peaks at 18, and won't burn out for a long, long time."[4]

MIDTEEN (Ages 16–17):
The Drive for Independence

> I wish my parents would start trusting me more and stop treating me like a little kid who still wears Pampers. I'm growing up. I can take care of myself.—Chad, 16

> I guess you could call me the more sensitive type. I'm not really into sports or the outdoors, and I prefer stuff like reading, writing, and art. But some guys make fun of me and call me a sissy. Is it okay if a guy doesn't act real macho?—Thomas, 16

> I'm almost a man, and I've never kissed a girl. I haven't even had a girlfriend. I feel creepy, like maybe I repulse females or something.—Nathan, 17

Driving, dating, a part-time job—like it or not, your little boy (who maybe now towers over you) is definitely growing up. And during this stage of development you're well aware that an "emotional war" between you and your son is in full swing. It's a perfectly normal part of growing up that psychologists describe as the "war of independence." With each step young people take on the path to adulthood, they become more and more independent of their mothers and fathers.

But in the meantime, how can you survive the daily storms on the home front? And when it comes to the specific needs of your teenage boy, what can you do to cool down the hot spots and even improve your relationship with him?

First, strive to understand the battle. A teenage boy in particular is very sensitive about personal injustice, self-worth, independence, privacy, and love. And whether or not he admits it, he's actually looking for boundaries. Some of his "testing behavior" is a way of him saying, "Do you care enough about me to keep me from doing this stupid thing? Do I have your attention? Are you concerned about who I am and what I'm doing?"

Second, understand a key that can help you over the barriers to solid conversation. This communication link I'm referring to is called *trust.* It's fragile and sometimes hard to build, but it's universally important.

Let's take a look at two ways trust can help you invade your high-schooler's world—without invading his space.

Trust earns you the right to be heard. Isn't "your right" already guaranteed simply by the fact that you're his parent? It should be, but in the real world it isn't. Your son is focused on the here and now. He's probably not thinking about all the sacrifices you've made for him through the years (or how much you love him). But he will, almost instantaneously, recall the "injustices" you've caused: your "countless broken promises," the times you blamed him for things he insists he didn't do, those days when you were "too busy." While perfect parenthood should never be your goal, it is important to build trust by earning the right to be heard. How? It starts with the next step.

Your attention builds trust. Teens know that love shown by parents says, "Your life is important, son, and I'm going to give you my time." When you spend time with him, show him you will listen and talk and work things out together. Invade his world . . . and let him invade yours.

LATE TEEN (Age 18+):
Launching Into the World

> I really want to figure out God's will for my life. Right now I have no idea what I'm going to do after high school. But I want my life to count. I want to make a difference in this world.—Zander, 18

> I'm in love with a girl who has all the qualities I'm looking for—including a strong faith in God. Even though we've only known each other for a month, I'm convinced that I've found my wife. We want to get married, but my parents are putting a stop to it. They say we're way too young to get serious romantically, especially to think about marriage. They want me to go to college first.—Josh, 19

> I'm really struggling with my identity. Who am I? A jock, a musician, a man of God? Things were actually pretty easy in high school and youth group. But now the thought of moving out on my own really terrifies me. Yet I can't live with my parents any longer. We fight a lot, and I really need my space.—John Mark, 18

By age eighteen, your son has reached the end of his teen years and has now approached yet another beginning: manhood.

His gaze is on the future and life on his own. But once he's independent of you, will he leave his faith back in high school, or will he strive to become the solid person God calls him to be? Will he fulfill his hopes and dreams, or will he slide toward a life of regrets?

It's a good time to remind him of a blessing—and a curse.

The Blessing: *Independence!* Those clashes with pesky siblings, constant ten p.m. curfews, and endless "Not while you're living under my roof" lectures become nothing more than murky adolescent memories.

The Curse: *Independence!* His parents, siblings, and youth minister aren't there to bail him out if he gets into trouble. The support system he once depended upon is now gone! (Or at least in a different state.)

Communicate this: "You—and only *you*—will be responsible for your actions. Making the right choices, and dealing with the wrong ones, is something you'll have to shoulder all by yourself. So, will you choose to bend the rules from time to time (knowing that you can), or will you commit to an unshakable faith in Christ?"

Now is the time for your son to decide. Like it or not, the days ahead will be filled with all kinds of temptations. But as his parent, you must let go and entrust his future to God.

What's Going On?
(The Five Stages of Puberty in Guys)

Your son's journey from boyhood to manhood is nothing short of a miracle. And as you already know, it happens in a hurry. In fact, most of his life you've probably used phrases like *growth spurt* to describe him: "I can't keep him in clothes and shoes because of his growth spurts."

Look out, because it's going to intensify with the onset of puberty. Some boys grow more than four inches in a single year.

During adolescence, the young man in your life is getting a new body and a new look: muscle growth, new hair scattered all over in some very adult places, not to mention zits. He'll also develop, if he hasn't already, a strong appetite for sex; this is a fact of life that way too many parents would rather avoid or deny. Along with his sexual awakening comes one of the more embarrassing aspects of being a teen guy: frequent erections. FYI—most boys are terrified by the possibility of experiencing an erection in public, especially in locker rooms and at swimming pools.

Bottom line: Your son will be extra sensitive about all these changes going on, so be patient, empathize with his awkward moments and crazy emotions, give him plenty of privacy, and never, ever make fun of the process. If you do, he'll shut down quicker than he can say "I'm outta here!"

Exactly what's going on with his body? Let's take a look at each stage of his development during the teen years:

Ages 9–11: Inside his body, male hormones are becoming active. They travel through the blood and give the testes the signal to begin the production of testosterone and sperm. Translation: When these hormones finish their work, he'll no longer think girls have cooties. In fact, he'll probably find himself very intrigued by cooties!

Ages 12–13: His testicles grow and begin hanging lower. Pubic hair appears at the base of his penis. Testosterone begins to transform the shape of his body. The muscles in his chest and shoulders grow bigger.

Ages 14–15: His penis gets longer and a little wider, and pubic hair gets darker and coarser. Facial and underarm hair may develop, as well as hair on his legs. His voice may begin to lower in pitch and may even crack at times. He'll experience his first ejaculation. He may actually be awakened some night by a "wet dream" (an ejaculation of semen from his penis). This can feel a little weird—probably not the kind of thing he'll want to talk about. Your job as a parent is to assure him that these things are absolutely normal.

Ages 16–17: He'll notice another growth spurt in his penis. More body hair appears and takes on an adult texture.

Ages 18–19: His body will reach full adult height and physique. Pubic hair spreads to his thighs and up toward his belly. Chest hair may appear, and shaving his growing facial hair is a must.

A Peek Inside the Masculine Mind

Unlike teenage girls, guys often struggle to express and process their moods. Too often they default to physical outbursts. Why?

First, let's go back in time a bit—actually, all the way back to your son's sixteenth through twenty-sixth weeks of fetal development.

Sometime during this stage, God "masculinized" his brain with testosterone so he could one day "think like a man." The result: Testosterone destroyed millions of fiber optics–like connections between his left-brain speech center and his right-brain feelings-emotions-beliefs region.

Here's how the process is explained by Donald M. Joy, PhD, professor of Human Development and Christian Education at Asbury Theological Seminary:

> Several interesting things happened to a boy's fetal brain as he was being created in his mother's womb. The mother's androgens combined with testosterone from the baby's developing testicles to form a frost-like, chemical coating on the entire left hemisphere of the boy's brain. The coating is God's way of "masculinizing" a boy. Consequently, men are able to "focus in" and give intense attention to anything, almost without distraction.[5]

Dr. Joy says this is why most boys have a tougher time putting their thoughts and feelings into words. It's also why many young males release emotions through intense, energetic bursts: They fly off the handle, slam doors, beat their fists on a wall, and lash out at their siblings. Then they shut down and retreat into some sort of focused activity, such as a computer game.

What's a Parent to Do?

Your testosterone-charged son is in yet another stage of his life—the high-octane teen years. And now he's beginning to "think like a man." What he desperately needs from you are clear parameters of right and wrong behavior.

Your son needs to learn from you the appropriate ways of processing his emotions and working through his struggles. But at the same time, he should never be forced to express himself in a way that's unnatural for him.

Here's a quick overview of how you can stay connected as your son navigates the rough waters of adolescence:

Let him retreat to his "cave." Guys need time alone in order to sort through a problem. Give him some space.

Let him talk when he's ready. Communicate that you are available to lend an ear.

Let him open up at his own pace. Never prod him to cough up every detail. This could cause him to shut down even more.

Let him know that his feelings are safe with you. This last step takes time and patience. But it's nurtured by you through an attitude of acceptance.

Remember: Everything Is Changing!

How a teen boy reacts to his changing body and journey into manhood depends on the reactions of family and friends and on his own personality. If your son knows what to expect, and if you have encouraged him to feel comfortable about changes in the way he looks and feels, he will probably take puberty in stride. If he enters puberty with high self-confidence, he's more likely to wind up pleased than embarrassed when his growing is done.

Here's a tremendous way you can help your teen: Try walking in his shoes. Take a moment to consider what life was like for you as a teenager. What aspect of your physical development did you find most embarrassing? How did you feel about it? Do you think your parents knew what was bothering you? Did they ever discuss it with you? Now think about the kind of involvement you would have liked to see from your parents.

Be sensitive to the changes going on in your son's life. As we stressed earlier, never make fun of physical developments such as height and weight. And never attempt to motivate your son through sarcasm or ridicule.

Above all, do your best to reduce the importance teens place on the body as the source of self-esteem. The fact is, our culture pays too much attention to people's physical appearance and not enough to other important skills and talents.

Listen to how one young man describes his teen years, as well as his survival secret:

> I hated my junior high years. Kids at school were brutal, and the teachers weren't much better. But my parents made a difference and my teen years got better.

My dad was there for me right when I needed him most, and my mom never stopped encouraging me. At the time, my friends were important to me, but they never replaced my parents. Consistently throughout my life, Mom and Dad told me that they loved me and that they were always there for me. Those messages really stuck with me—especially when my friends pressured me to do stuff that was wrong.

Instead of getting myself into a stupid situation, I'd go to my parents for advice. I trust what they say and know that they'll help me make good decisions. I owe everything to Mom and Dad.—Sean, 19

CHAPTER 2

Breaking the Code of Cruelty

The next time you set foot on your son's school campus or visit his youth group, look around you. What will you see? Cliques. Herds of guys and girls who never seem to cross an invisible line that separates the classes.

The cool kids claim one part of the room. And the preppies, serious kids, skaters, surfers, computer kids, and druggies each claim their own space.

It's not fair—and it can even be downright cruel—but the sad truth is, your son has been sized up, labeled, and forced into a rigid social group. And every day he must survive a hostile world that consists of bullies and the *bullied*; one in which the strong prey upon the weak.

Too often, guys retreat to a prison of loneliness. They feel trapped and terrified, so they hide their emotions behind tough masks, never flinching and always fearing humiliation from their peers.

It's a lethal mix. Just ask fifteen-year-old Andrew.

Endless teasing. Constant humiliation. Andrew was at his breaking point. He lay on the ground by a basketball court—buckled like a crumpled, discarded Pepsi can.

"You're a total loser," taunted one of the boys who hit him.

"Don't even think about shooting hoops with us," shouted another. "We're way out of your league, dork."

Suddenly a whistle blew, and the boys scattered—leaving Andrew alone.

"What's this all about, son?" barked the school's coach.

Andrew raised his head and tried to blink away the tears. "They hate me," he mumbled. "Everybody hates me 'cause I'm skinny and clumsy . . . and not a jock."

"Look, sports just isn't your thing," the coach responded, helping Andrew to his feet. "Don't sweat the teasing. Just be a man, tough it out, and keep going."

Andrew's head began to swim. *If this is manhood, then I don't want it. Something MUST change!*

Bullying is a cruel reality on many school campuses, even in church youth groups. It's not fun. And it's not harmless, regardless of what some people say.

"The constant teasing literally crushed my confidence," says Andrew, who is now in college—and who desperately wants to protect his future kids from bullying. "Back then, all I heard from coaches, teachers, and parents was the same thing: 'Just ignore it. Teasing is a part of growing up.' I felt trapped and alone, yet I kept telling myself, 'Something *must* give.'"

In today's hostile guy culture, boys must endure a world characterized by hurtfulness and shame, one in which it is more important to fit in at any cost than to care or to understand.

Take fifteen-year-old David, for example. This kid is a talented artist who dreams about one day becoming president of his own comic book company—or maybe even filling an upscale New York art gallery with *his* masterpieces. Yet he feels as if every other guy at his school cares about only one thing: scoring at the next party. Despite being excited about his future and all the possibilities God has set before him, he can't help noticing that too many other boys his age put on cynical acts, making everyone think that nothing but the moment really matters.

"Here's the crazy thing," David says. "I catch myself wondering if something is wrong with *me.* Some guys call me 'geek' or 'church boy.' It really hurts. Why do kids have to be so cruel?"

Bullying is abuse, not child's play. And as Andrew so wisely put it, "Something *must* change."

Here's what other guys are telling us. . . .

How can I get a bully at school to leave me alone? This kid has been bothering me for about a month, and I'm tired of it. You see, because of a bad accident that pierced my bladder when I was nine, I have to wear bladder protection. This guy at school saw me taking a wet Depends off in a bathroom stall, and he hasn't let it go since. He taunts me in the halls, calling me names like Diaper Boy and Big Baby! I told the principal, and he said there was nothing he could do unless he had proof. So the next day, I used my cell phone to secretly video this kid harassing me. The principal suspended him for three days, and everything was fine until he came back. He was furious and started hitting me and telling everyone about my diapers, and he even pulled down my pants to prove it! I was so upset. But the Bible always gives examples of resolving things in other ways besides violence. And my mom always gives me the violence-isn't-the-answer lecture. But I dread going to school. I really can't handle this, yet I don't know what to do.—Josh, 14

I'm one of the smartest kids at my school, according to my friends. But there's this kid who hounds me and makes fun of me for being a nerd. What's worse, one of my so-called friends sticks up for his antics. I've asked my parents for help, and I've talked to my principal. Also, I've been praying and asking God for help, but I'm not getting any answers. Please, please, please . . . HELP ME!—Abraham, 15

I've been told by my parents and youth leader to pray for a bully. Recently, I gave it a try. During lunch at school, I caught up with this boy who has been teasing me. I sat right across from him and said, "Can I pray for you?" That caused all his friends to laugh, so he got up, grabbed me by the collar, and started dragging me toward the garbage can. In my head I thought, I can't let this happen. So I decked him. That was a bad, bad idea. He came right after me, and I ran, but he caught up and put me in the trash can. Then he punched me and said, "Hit me again and see what happens, you Bible freak!" I was crushed. I tried to do something right, but it went wrong.—James, 13

I have a HUGE problem with bullies. This one kid constantly picks on me. It feels like torture, and I can't take it anymore. Pleeeease, can someone help me break out of the fear I deal with every day?!—Chad, 13

A former friend of mine has posted an online threat to me and two of my very good friends. He did this on MySpace. We all feel very threatened by this email, and our parents have decided to go to the school officials about this problem. But what else can we do? We don't want to draw attention to ourselves.—Karl, 15

Bullies and Victims

Bestselling author Frank Peretti, who wrote a book on bullying titled *No More Victims,* is among what he calls the world's "walking wounded." He warns parents to (1) take bullying seriously, and (2) put a stop to it now! He told *Breakaway* magazine,

> At some point in a child's life he becomes the inferior one, the different one, the ugly one, the fat one. For whatever reason that shapes the way he or she interacts. . . . It's like painting a sign around your neck: "Beat up on me because you'll get away with it." You begin to expect to be treated that way, and the other kids pick up on that like an animal smelling prey.
>
> That's how it was for me. My teen world was a virtual prison. Here's some advice for Christians of all ages: Have nothing to do with words that wound.[1]

According to family therapists, there are two basic types of male bullies. One is the boy who feels inadequate, so he tries to elevate himself by picking on others. Perhaps he is an underachiever or is dealing with trouble in the home front. The other kind of bully is the type many parents overlook: the successful kid. Often good students, athletes, or Christian kids who seem to have everything going for them fall into a trap of thinking that bullying is "the cool thing to do," especially with friends.

Unplugging the Pain

Is your son a victim of bullying and teasing? Know the warning signs:

- **Isolation:** Is he spending more and more time alone? Has he lost his interest in school and peers?
- **Depression:** Is your son detached emotionally? Is he more irritable than usual? Does he appear to be increasingly tired or sullen?
- **Low Self-Confidence:** Is your teen down on himself? Does he speak negatively about his appearance or his abilities?

Give him this advice:

- **Avoid danger.** Proverbs 22:3 says that "a prudent man sees danger and takes refuge." In contrast, "the simple keep going and suffer for it." This translates into common sense. But what if a bully is strutting in your son's direction? This leads to the next step. . . .
- **Talk confidently.** Proverbs 15:1 says "a gentle answer turns away wrath." The other half of that verse points out that "a harsh word stirs up anger." Encourage your son to make every effort to diffuse a situation. How? With a direct, calm answer: "Look, I don't have a problem with you. I'm going now."
- **Walk away.** Romans 12:17–18 says, "Do not repay anyone evil for evil. Be careful to do what is right in the eyes of everybody. If it is possible, as far as it depends on you, live at peace with everyone." Walking away—instead of

standing there arguing at the top of his lungs—is the best way to maintain peace.

What You Can Do

- **Don't tolerate bullying.** Never dismiss it as harmless teenage behavior or as a "hardening experience" that will prepare your son for adulthood.
- **Create a safe harbor where your son can retreat.** Let him know that you take his dilemma seriously and that you care. Encourage him to build a "shield of friends"—likeminded adults and peers who will stand by his side.
- **Build his confidence.** Remind him of his positive qualities, and communicate daily the messages he desperately needs to hear: "You are normal," "I believe in you," "Your life counts," "You make me so proud."
- **Help him consider the words of his mouth.** Ask your son, "Does your speech encourage and empower—or does it wound and destroy? Do you communicate hope, or do you occasionally spew hateful insults and put-downs at others?"
- **Point your teen to Psalm 19:14:** "May the words of my mouth and the meditation of my heart be pleasing in your sight, O Lord, my Rock and my Redeemer."
- **Encourage him to be a defender of the weak.** But caution your son to avoid being foolhardy. If there's a chance of violence if he intervenes, instruct him to go to a teacher or the principal. Let him know that it's not snitching; it's helping a classmate. It also shows real courage.

If Your Son Is a Bully

For countless junior and senior high guys, an hour of gym class is sixty minutes of absolute torment. Getting slammed up against lockers, snapped with wet towels, and pelted with merciless name-calling is a daily experience.

And all too often the adults in their lives look the other way. Coaches, teachers—even parents—shrug their shoulders, claiming, "It's just a normal, teen-guy thing. If boys can tough it out, they'll be the better for it."

We can't stress it enough: There's nothing normal or harmless about bullying. The pain of a put-down can wound a kid for life. And some guys who are teased turn into bullies themselves. Steer your son clear of this cycle. He must understand that hate begets hate, which only continues the ugly pattern. Instead, help him to be the one who builds others up.

If you suspect that your son is a bully, take these steps:

- Have a talk with him. Find out why he feels a need to pick on other kids. Help him to understand the harm he is doing.

- Encourage your son to find friends who like him for who he is—not who they think he should be.

- Fuel his imagination. Get him excited about the future and all the possibilities ahead of him: the things he can experience, the places he can go, the man he can become.

- Help him to live beyond the moment—to dream big and to explore all the possibilities that await him.

Three Ways to Deflate the Pressure

Handling bullies' peer fear begins long before the pressure hits. In other words, wise guys make up their minds ahead of time how they're going to react to the temptations that will arise. Encourage your son to prepare now for the battles ahead.

Accountability is the key. This means having a friend or two who will check up on his commitment to Christ. Ecclesiastes 4:12 says single strands of rope are weak on their own, but three woven together will stay tight and strong.

Show him the big picture. The pressure to fit in with the crowd at any cost may seem unbearable at this stage of your teen's life. But ask him to consider this important question: "Will it matter in five years what the popular crowd thinks of you? Will it matter what God thinks of you?" Encourage him to examine Philippians 3:12–14 and discover the importance of focusing on the finish line, not the stumbling blocks around him.

Teach him to count the cost. Actions have consequences, which are not always fair. Help your teen think about how a choice now might impact his plans, his family, his future wife and kids. Ask him, "Will a choice you face put you in physical danger? Will you risk emotional damage? Is momentary acceptance from the crowd worth destroying your future?"

CHAPTER 3

"Eight Things I Need You to Know About Me"

A teen girl can talk your ear off. She can rattle on and on about anything and everything. I (Susie) watched a teen girl, Tara, on one of our missions trips. We were riding the bus from the airport to our hotel in Lima, Peru, and she talked the ear off of the person sitting next to her. After that person fell asleep, Tara simply turned to the window and kept talking!

Maybe you're thinking, *I'd give anything to hear my son talk that much!* Let's face it: Most teen guys simply aren't as verbal, open, or desirous to share their thoughts and feelings. So while your son may never tell you what he'd love for you to know about him, here are eight important things he *does* want you to know . . . and not only *know,* but truly understand about him.

"I'm Visual"

> Whenever my dad wants to talk to me, I know it's going to be boring. He just goes on and on and on . . . about whatever. I act like I'm paying attention, but I really couldn't care less. Even the sound of his voice makes me sleepy. How come family conversations are never exciting?—Thad, 14

You already know this, but here's a quick recap: Guys are wired so much differently from girls! Guys are visual; girls are connected through emotions. It doesn't take much to turn a guy on. It also doesn't take much to lure him into being interested in something. When something's presented to him in a fast-paced, high-tech, color-exploding visual manner, he's easily drawn in.

So to communicate most effectively with your son, try to relate in visual terms. We know you can't bring out the fog machines and turn on a spotlight for every conversation, but try to create visual word pictures when talking with him. If he can imagine it, you'll get through to him a lot faster.

This can work especially well when having family devotions and making a spiritual application. Let's say your son is hanging around with some friends who aren't the best influence on him. You're concerned, but he keeps saying, "Don't worry about it. I'm not doing the stuff they do. I've never even tasted alcohol."

Of course, you're wondering how long that will last, and you desperately want him to learn how easily the wrong kind of friends could pull him down. So at family devotions one evening, you ask him to read some Scriptures you've chosen ahead of time about influence and the importance of making wise choices and not compromising. (Proverbs is a great book for this.)

Place a kitchen chair in the middle of the room and ask your son to stand on it. You sit on the floor in front of the chair. Ask your son to pull you up. He may or may not be able to do it as he continues to stand in the chair. After a minute has passed, pull him out of the chair. Make the application: "While you *say* you want to influence your friends, keep in mind that it's much easier for someone to pull you down than for you to pull him up." Because you've communicated with him visually, your son will remember this lesson far longer than if you had simply lectured him.

"I'd Rather Experience a Lesson Than Hear One"

> I learn more when I get to experience the lesson—not just hear about it. I get bored with lectures and Bible studies. Instead, give me a hands-on task. Let me roll up my sleeves and get dirty. That's when stuff really sticks with me.—Andrew, 15

Really good youth pastors know this secret. And instead of simply telling Bible stories, they help their students experience them. For example, I (Susie) used to be a youth pastor, and instead of simply talking about the bread and fish one Wednesday night, I advertised that the first five thousand students who showed up would be treated to fish and chips. This way they could actually taste the fish as we talked about the miracle. They could imagine more easily having a bunch of bread left over after they were so stuffed with chips they couldn't eat any more.

Instead of simply telling your son that we're to be the hands and feet of Jesus and to be involved in ministry, why not take him to your local soup kitchen or rescue mission to "get his hands dirty"? Volunteer to help those less fortunate by serving them. Or consider participating with him on a missions trip. I take approximately five hundred teens and adults on a two-week international missions trip every summer. Each year we have parents who come as leaders and get to experience a life-changing event with their son or daughter. Go to *susiemag.com* and click on the "Never the Same Missions" link for information.

I've seen it happen again and again: Once students see true poverty face-to-face—once they *experience* it—the reality crawls underneath their skin and right into their hearts. When they've seen people living in cardboard boxes, they will think twice before complaining about what Mom is making for dinner or about having to clean their room.

"I Have a Fragile Ego Despite My Tough Exterior"

I'm from a Christian home, but my parents and family always call me names or try to label me. Why can't they build me up, not tear me down? My dad says I'm lazy. My mom used to call me a stone heart. My bro has had issues with me since childhood. They don't give me a chance, and this really hurts.—Chaz, 18

Guys may act tough on the outside, because the media says that's what being a man is, but they hurt on the inside just like girls do. Guys may be better at hiding their emotions, but they still feel.

All it takes is for one person to make fun of a guy, and he's ruined for the rest of the day. Again, he may not show it, but he's dying on the inside. This is why it's so important that parents not be sarcastic with their son and not tease him.

Fourteen-year-old Logan had a medium build and average looks. But his older sister teased him by calling him ugly. "Hi, ugly. Wanna go get a burger with me?" "Hey, ugly! Where's the remote?" This went on for years. And even though Logan knew his sister loved him, he never felt attractive to the opposite sex until he was in a relationship with a wonderful Christian girl in college who consistently affirmed him.

Even though Derrick was seventeen, his dad continued to call him Little Dummy. It was a nickname he'd given Derrick when he was three, because he struggled with saying the letter R correctly. Even though Derrick was no dummy, he grew up resenting his dad and felt inferior to his siblings regarding school.

Your job as a parent is to build up, encourage, and affirm your son. We've said it before, but let's repeat it again: NEVER NEVER NEVER EVER be sarcastic or tease your son! You may not discover until years later the extent of your damage to his ego that teasing and sarcasm can cause.

Instead, consciously choose to affirm your son in as many areas as possible. Does he have good penmanship? Tell him! His hair looks good today? Let him know. His friends enjoy his company? Brag on him about that. My (Susie's) parents did this for my brother and me. As a result, I grew up thinking I could do and become anything I wanted. I felt as though nothing was out of reach for me. It certainly wasn't because I was more talented than those around me; it was simply because my parents instilled confidence in me that in turn helped me to have a strong and positive self-esteem. Do the same for your son!

"I Need to Be Close to God"

I come from a Christian home, but I don't have a close relationship with Jesus Christ. In fact, I'm finding it very, very hard to open up to Him and pray—yet I feel a strong need to get things right spiritually.

I just don't sense God in my life. When I pray, I feel like I'm just talking to myself. My youth pastor gave me a bunch of happy talk and pat answers. He also gave me some Bible verses to read. (To be honest, I think he cares more about packing kids in on Wednesday nights and putting on glitzy programs than he does about connecting with teens.)

I guess you could say that I'm kind of a spiritual mess. I'm not very close to Jesus, I don't understand the Bible, I don't feel like I fit in at church . . . and most Christian kids I know don't seem any different from so-called "worldly" ones. So I'm starting to ask myself this question: "How can Christianity really make a difference for me?"—Brandon, 16

My church's Bible study has been talking about defeating temptations. I was thinking today, if we have a temptation and fall into it, God will forgive us. What, then, would keep us from using that as an excuse? When considering whether to do the right or the wrong thing, you could just say, "Oh, God will forgive me, so why not?"—Darius, 14

I really want to be a man of God and follow His will for my life. The events of last summer solidified this desire in me. (I guess I needed a spiritual nudge!) Let me tell you about it.

I went on a missions trip to a camp where they bus kids from a horrible city in Pennsylvania. Every day during the summer, Christians get them away from the horrible environment of drugs and violence and teach them the hope of Jesus.

Getting involved with this ministry changed my life. I've come to realize that I can't run from God anymore, and I can't ignore Him. I was spiritually dead, and now I am growing. I'm writing this letter to ask you to pray for me and to pray for those little children and all the little kids around the world. They suffer the most—yet they are our future.—Daniel, 17

With the vast differences between Catholics, Baptists, Presbyterians, nondenominationals, etc., I find it hard to discern what the actual message of the Bible is. Any tips on how I can focus on God and not on what each "faction" tries to get me to believe?—Eric, 15

Lately, I've been wondering why I believe in God. Like, when people ask me why I do, I can't think of an answer for them. Is there any solid proof that there really is a God? Usually when I ask somebody this question, they tell me that He's done many miracles in people's lives, but couldn't this be some kind of psychological thing? For example, I've read that doctors have a pill that will do nothing, but they tell their patients that the pill will make them better. So somebody with a headache, stomachache, or anything else would take the pill, and because they're so sure it will work, they start feeling better.

Couldn't this be the same thing with God? People just convince themselves that God has healed them, and they're healed. Also, is there proof that the Bible is really true? Couldn't somebody just have made up a story, turned it into a book, and people believed it, kind of like The Da Vinci Code?—Samuel, 17

For the past year I've been on a quest to get closer to God, striving to live my life as Jesus did. I know that I'll never be able to follow the exact steps Christ took, which was to live a perfect life, but I can always try. I need more wisdom in doing so. I pray and read the Bible, but it's not ringing the bell. I'm not sure what to do. Am I praying right? What could I be doing wrong? I'm feeling overwhelmed.—Sam, 14

In my church we've been watching the documentary Expelled: No Intelligence Allowed. Here's a recap: The academic world is cracking down on people who speak about intelligent design. The makers of the documentary repeatedly say that it's like a wall; you're allowed to say whatever you want as long as you have an opinion on one side of the wall, and in this case that's for evolution. But as soon as you say something on the other side of the wall—in this case, for intelligent design—you're in trouble and get the boot. The producers also repeatedly stated that because we live in America, we should have the freedom to voice our beliefs and opinions.

This is what bothers me: If we say we should have freedom to teach intelligent design in schools, then why can't there be homosexual marriages or abortions, etc.? I totally don't agree with homosexual marriage or abortion, but to say they can't do that is like putting up a wall (the same thing the creators of Expelled are fighting against). On one side, you can be against that, but as soon as you go on the other side of the wall you get in trouble.—John, 16

We purposefully included a lot of letters in this section because we want to overemphasize how important it is that you be a godly role model to your son. If he doesn't see Christ in your life, he may reject Christianity.

Determine to do whatever it takes to guide your son into a healthy relationship with Christ. Do you realize the most important job you have as a parent is to disciple your children?

Do you realize the most important job you have as a parent is to disciple your children?

Do you realize the most important job you have as a parent is to disciple your children?

That's not a printing mistake. We want to say it again. We'll make it a bit more personal, and we invite you to read it out loud this time: *The most important job I have is to disciple my children!*

Making money, securing the right job, finding a nice home, setting aside a college fund, cooking healthy meals, coaching Little League, helping them soar in academics, music, drama, sports . . . *nothing* is as important as discipling your children!

Please allow us to be blunt: Are you discipling your son into becoming a man after God's own heart? Are you reading the Bible with him? Do you pray together consistently? (And no, a quick prayer at the table before dinner isn't what we're talking about.) Are you introducing him to spiritual heroes through missionary books and the history of your church? Have you shown him how to actually study the Bible? Does he have more than one translation of the Bible? Are you helping him memorize Scripture? Is he reading good Christian books? What about Christian classics such as *Pilgrim's Progress* by John Bunyan, *Hinds' Feet on High Places* by Hannah Hurnard, *Absolute Surrender* by Andrew Murray, *In His Steps* by Charles Sheldon, *The Screwtape Letters* by C.S. Lewis, *A Plain Account of Christian Perfection* by John Wesley, *My Utmost for His Highest* by Oswald Chambers?

If your son is doubting Christianity or the Bible being true, we recommend the student editions of *The Case for Christ* and

The Case for Faith, both by Lee Strobel. If your son is asking about creationism and evolution, grab *The Case for a Creator.* Again, make sure you get the student editions. They're short and easy to understand.

If your son isn't being exposed to the above, why not?

There's nothing else in the world more important than discipling your child.

"I Need You to Be Close and Listen"

I told my mom about my porn problem, but she went insane. I just need her to hear me—and help, not reject me. She has to understand that I'm a guy. I struggle with different stuff than girls do. I'm made differently. I really need a guy to connect with. My mom just doesn't understand me.—Wyatt, 16

Genuinely listening to your son involves time and investment. When was the last time the two of you did something together—just the two of you? Make it a priority to establish a weekly "date" with your son . . . a special time the two of you can get together and talk about anything.

Go fishing, get coffee, simply drive to the gas station together and fill up all the cars in the family, set up the tent and camp overnight in the backyard, toss a baseball back and forth, go out for burgers, make a pizza, clean out the garage together, unroll the sleeping bags and spend the night on the living room floor. It doesn't have to be expensive or extravagant, but make time to be with your son to give him your undivided attention.

And when he talks, let him know you really *are* listening. You can do that by repeating part of what he's saying and asking him a question about it. Here's an example:

Dad: So how was gym class today? Was Jake there?

Charlie: Uh . . . okay, I guess. Yeah, Jake was there. He's still telling everyone I'm gay just 'cause I haven't done it with a girl.

Dad: How does that make you feel?

Charlie: How do you think? Stupid. Lousy. Ostracized. Alone. Picked on.

Dad: Do you realize, though, that you've made the right decision to remain sexually pure until marriage?

Charlie: Yep. I know that. But when guys like Jake won't let up, it sure makes me think twice.

Dad: I think I'm hearing you say that because you're being bullied, you're thinking twice about your commitment to purity. Is that right?

Charlie: Well, yeah. And no. I mean, yeah, I think about it. What guy doesn't? But I know what's right.

Dad: Let's spend some time praying about it tonight, okay?

Charlie: Yeah, whatever. I need all the help I can get.

Dad: Feeling pretty beat up right now, aren't you?

Charlie: No kidding.

Dad: Hey, Charlie, I never get tired of telling you how proud I am of you! Your mom and I love the man you're becoming.

Charlie: Oh, Dad! *(Please keep going.)*

Dad: Seriously! Lots of guys would've caved by now. We're proud of your morals. You know we're crazy about you, right?

Charlie: Yeah.

Listening—genuinely listening—will give your son tons of security during these growing years.

"I Yearn for Adventure"

Every guy needs adventure. Determine to set aside at least one week each year for a family vacation. My (Susie's) dad was really big on this. He made sure that we had a vacation every single year (as long as my brother and I were living at home).

We weren't rolling in money, but my parents were wise and knew how to budget. They carefully set aside money each month for a weeklong family vacation every August.

I would have been happy staying at home and going swimming every day, but they understood the importance of adventure to my brother, Kent. So each summer they planned an amazing adventure and lifelong memories for us.

One summer we visited Mount Rushmore. Another summer we camped out in the Black Hills. And another summer we camped all the way from Oklahoma City to Montreal, Canada, stopping at national parks along the way. Our parents took us to national sightseeing places, took photographs, taught us the meaning of what we saw, and made sure my brother got the adventures he needed.

We had a Ping-Pong table my whole life. Every Sunday after church, my dad and Kent would venture to the game room and have it out in extensive Ping-Pong matches. Dad taught him to slam the ball, and I'd hear them yelping and hollering until Mom called everyone to Sunday dinner. They understood their son needed adventure.

I was in grade school when Dad set up a tetherball and pole in the backyard. He and Kent would play every evening when Dad came home.

When my brother was in high school, my mom told my dad she thought we should get a pool table. She explained that Kent just needed to have something fun at home. What a wise mom! She understood the necessity of adventure for a guy, and she also knew that if we had a pool table, Kent and all his friends would be at our place instead of someplace she didn't know about.

Every guy needs adventure. It may be a rousing game of chess, or it may be learning to hunt. It could be helping to build an extra room onto the house, or it may be planting a tomato garden in the backyard. But every boy needs adventure. Strive to help your son get what he needs.

"I Need My Space"

Every guy needs his alone time. Please learn to trust him enough to give it to him. And if he breaks your trust and does something he shouldn't during his time of "space"? Then pull in the reins and watch him more closely until he can earn that alone time again.

Jay had always done well in English classes, and during his sophomore year of high school, he discovered he was a pretty good writer. He was on the school newspaper staff and had plenty of opportunities to write. In sophomore English that year, he discovered all kinds of poetry: free verse, haiku, sonnets. His parents admired the high grades he was receiving but couldn't understand why he spent so much time in his room.

They kept the computer in the family office, so they knew he wasn't online, but what was he doing? His mom finally approached him. "Jay, why are you in your room so much? Come out and join us in the family room."

After a few weeks of prodding, Jay finally opened his desk drawer the next time his mom knocked on his door. He pulled out a huge journal and said, "Mom, there's so much stuff inside of me. I feel like I'm gonna explode if I don't do something with it. So I just write stuff, you know?"

"What are you writing?"

"Just stuff. Sometimes it's a poem. Last night I started a mystery. Tonight I've just been journaling."

"Can't you write in the family room?"

"No, Mom! It's too full. I mean, the TV's on, or someone's talking. I just have to be alone with this. I need you to understand."

His wise mom knew Jay had talent and didn't want to squelch it, but she also wanted him to know they desired some family time with him. "Okay, Jay. We want you to spend more time with us. But I also want you to have the time you need to express yourself and develop the obvious talent God has given you. So here's what we'll do: You can spend one hour every night in your room, door closed, writing. I'll make sure no one in the family bothers you. And you choose when you want the hour. Before dinner, after dinner, whenever. But you also have to spend some time with us in the family room."

Jay agreed. And as a college student now majoring in journalism, he's grateful for a mom who gave him the space he needed.

Your son may not be into journalism. Maybe he needs time alone in the garage to tinker with an engine. Or perhaps he wants time alone to lift weights in the spare bedroom. Give him boundaries, but also be willing to give him the space he needs.

"I May Not Talk a Lot, but I Hear You"

I (Susie) spent some time recently with a couple who said their son, Marcus, didn't speak until he was three. They were worried and thought he might be autistic. It really surprised me, because Marcus hasn't stopped talking since I've known him! I turned to him and said, "You just didn't have anything to say, did you, Marcus? Just taking it all in."

While they'll never really know the reason he didn't talk, Marcus truly does have a big intake ability. So do lots of other guys.

Studies indicate women use 30,000 to 50,000 words, while men use only 20,000 to 25,000. Women simply use more words than men.

But guys just don't have the need to talk as much as girls do. Girls have to talk and love to hear themselves talk. Guys can process things inwardly and be happy never to voice what they've just thought through. Girls have to tell the world.

But don't let your son's quietness fool you. He's actually taking in much more than you realize. That's why it's important for you to carefully weigh your words—what you say and how you say it. Guys are sensitive, and they *will* take what you say and turn it over inside their minds.

Guys are less likely to juggle more than one thing at once, though. So if your son is watching a football game, understand this isn't the right time to discuss how he feels about space travel or the stimulus program.

CHAPTER 4

Teen Guy Battlegrounds

"Why do I get blamed for EVERYTHING?!" your son screams from the top of his lungs.

You cross your arms and lock eyes with him. "Watch your tone, young man," you say in a low, stern voice. "You're not *always* blamed, but you are the oldest in this family—and you know better. I want you to set a good example."

Suddenly you sense movement behind you. Your younger son has taken cover behind you, and you don't have to turn around to know he's silently antagonizing his older brother again.

"Did you see that?" your older son gasps. "Maggot is doing it again."

"Oh, give it a rest," you respond. "Why can't you two get along? Why do you insist on turning our house into a battle zone?"

Your teen son gasps again. Just before slamming his bedroom door, he launches one last missile: "Not only is Maggot treated better, but you and Dad let him get away with murder."

Once inside his room, your son flops on his bed and buries his face in his pillow. He's convinced that you conceived his little brother just to spy on him.

"He's like a miniature Secret Service agent," your son grumbles to himself. "Just when I thought I could trust him, he tells Mom what I did last week—and I get grounded for the next three years. And as Mom pronounces punishment, that ever-so-faint smile plays across Maggot's lips. Oh, if I could just get my hands on those lips."

Your son flops on his bed and begins to throw a Nerf ball against his Colorado Rockies poster.

"'No-o-o-o-o,'" he mumbles in his best prison-warden voice. "'You *can't* have that, you *can't* go there, you *can't* hang out with those friends!' When will they learn I'm not a little kid anymore?"

During supper he had barely said two sentences—one of which was "Pass the potatoes—please." When his homework was completed, he didn't watch TV with the family. Instead, he shut his bedroom door and lost himself in his music.

Meanwhile, you collapse in the easy chair and squeeze your eyes shut. *Why do we go through this every time I say the word* no? you ask yourself as you replay the argument in your head. *Why do I always come off as the prison warden? Why can't we have a peaceful relationship?*

Both of these are all-too familiar scenes between boys and their parents, yet we can't help but wonder . . .

How is it possible for a houseful of people to love each other so much—yet at times feel as if they can't stand each other?

Why is it that we can live under the same roof with our spouses, sons, and daughters and be so close to them—which means we know all of their strange quirks—yet sometimes feel like complete strangers?

The answer is obvious: An emotional war has erupted between many parents and teens. It's that "war of independence," a perfectly normal phase of growing up. With each step the young man in your life takes on the path to adulthood, he becomes more and more independent of Mom and Dad.

But in the meantime, how can you survive the daily storms on your home front? And when it comes to the specific needs of boys, what can you do to cool down the hot spots and even improve your relationship with him? Here are a few ideas:

Allow for a cooling-off period. Unless you detect some serious disrespect, a little bit of the cold-shoulder treatment from him won't hurt. True, it doesn't feel too good, but he needs a chance to cool off and process the situation. (For that matter, you need to cool off as well.) Give him time to cool off, but . . .

Don't let him shut down for too long. Too much of the cold-shoulder treatment and you could end up with even more tension later on. After a fair amount of time has passed, make an effort to get your teen talking about the disagreement. Communicating and listening will ultimately open the doors to greater understanding.

Let him know that he is on your "most wanted" list. Say something like this: "If you feel as though you're on our 'most wanted' list, you're right! Regardless of all the conflicts we experience together, you really are *wanted* by us. We really do love you."

Now let's focus our attention on some universal home-front hot spots. We'll examine the intricacies of each of these tension zones as well as solutions to those tiring fights.

Sibling Storms (A Sensible Remedy)

You're well aware that sibling rivalry is a fact of family life—a difficult fact that can intensify the moment your teen hits puberty. Yet few things can cause a parent to become a raving maniac quicker than constant bickering and fighting.

So what's the answer? Is it possible to defuse the constant missiles your children launch at each other? Can you actually teach your teenage son to be a peacemaker? We think you can. While you'll never eliminate sibling rivalry, it is possible to improve your teen's attitude, foster mutual respect, and save *your* sanity.

Before the Storm: Promote a Peaceful Environment

Help him understand the conflict. As a teenager, your son is very sensitive about personal injustice, self-worth, independence, privacy, and love. The next time he's veering toward a head-on collision with a sibling, encourage him to take three steps: (1) cool down, (2) identify the problem, and (3) talk it out.

Teach him to be a problem solver. Help your son realize that when two people have trouble getting along, it's usually because a problem has built up over time. So if trust is the hot-button issue with a family member, he must get to the root of the problem. Say this: "Talk calmly with the one who wronged you and figure out how the conflict began. And as you confront your brother or sister, avoid assigning fault. Instead, concentrate on finding a solution to your problem."

Steer him away from sarcasm. Tell him: "One of the easiest ways to do battle is to make fun of your brother or sister, but it's also one of the most damaging. Cruel remarks have a tendency to hurt others deeply, and the wounds will keep on giving pain long after the issue has been settled."

Encourage him to show respect. Not only will his family members return it, they'll also become less prone to quarreling with him. They'll even let him have his way from time to time.

After the Storm: Set Clear Boundaries

Help him avoid a "bitterness burn." Tell your son: "Bitterness hurts you far more than it hurts others. It's like a hot coal. The longer and tighter it is held, the deeper the burn. Bitterness can leave scars that even time cannot erase."

Encourage him to fight his own battles. Tell him: "Don't report every little disagreement to me. After you've cooled off, sit down with your brother or sister and figure out how to settle the conflict on your own."

Teach him to forgive—then forgive again. Tell him: "Think of all the ways you feel you have been wronged by your brother or sister. Then work toward genuine forgiveness. Understand that forgiveness is not denying that you've been hurt, or even trying to understand why a person has acted a certain way. Genuine forgiveness involves consciously choosing to release the hurt someone has caused—and continuing to love that person. Can you get to this point with the family member who has wronged you?"

Clear Up Parent-Teen Static

Conversation No. 1—How It Could Be ...

Teenage Son: "I hate my English composition class, and I don't see the point in taking it. It's not like I'm gonna be a novelist someday."

Parent: "I hear you—writing can be hard. But, you know, I'm glad I stuck with it when I was your age. Is there any way I can help?"

Teenage Son: "I have to write a two-page theme paper tonight. Got any suggestions for a topic?"

Parent: "Have a seat, and let's see what we can dream up together."

Teenage Son: "Thanks. This really takes a load off my mind."

Conversation No. 2—How It Usually Is ...

Teenage Son: "I hate my English composition class, and I don't see the point in taking it. It's not like I'm gonna be a novelist someday."

Parent: "I don't want to hear another complaint out of you. English is a requirement. Now get up to your room and do your homework."

Teenage Son: "You never listen to me when I have a problem. I can't wait till I'm on my own and don't have to put up with stupid rules."

Parent: "Keep it up, smart mouth, and you'll get yourself grounded."

Teenage Son: "This stinks. You are absolutely ruining my life."

So which conversation is typical with your son? Let us guess—the second one! Too bad, because Conversation No. 1 isn't that far out of touch with reality. In fact, with some work, it can actually be the regular mode of conversation. But it all begins with an important nine-letter word: LISTENING.

"My parents just don't listen to me" is the anthem of many teen boys. Likewise, it's a complaint echoed by parents: "I can't get through to him—he just won't listen."

Listening is where effective communication really begins. Instead of engaging in a verbal tug-of-war with your son, follow these essential steps:

Begin with passive listening (or silence). Give your son a chance to speak his mind. "I'm just not getting anything out of band and really want to drop out. I can't keep up, and the teacher always embarrasses me in front of everyone."

Give acknowledgment responses. Don't just stand there with a blank expression on your face. Even when you're listening passively, it's a good idea to make sincere comments such as "I see" or "Oh?" that emphasize that you are paying attention.

Offer a "door opener." This is a simple, nonjudgmental statement, such as, "How would you feel about talking to the teacher after class? Maybe she'll ease up on you." How-you-feel questions are less threatening to your son, and they help spark communication.

Exercise active listening with a communication style called "shared meaning." Here's how it works:

- You're frustrated because your son didn't clean his room before the dinner party, not to mention the mess he made on the patio. So you approach him and say, "We need to talk about this. I'd like you to hear my side."
- Once you have his attention, you explain your point of view (which you've thought through ahead of time) without being interrupted.
- Next, your son repeats what he heard you say.
- You then clarify or confirm what he said, ensuring that your thoughts and feelings have been heard accurately.
- The process continues with him sharing his point of view, and you listening and repeating what he said.

The goal of shared meaning is to be heard accurately. And once you've had a chance to state your case and listen to his, the foundation is set for communication—and for a fair solution to the problem at hand. A solution that's grounded on listening and being heard . . . not just another pointless Tuesday night fight.

Personal Taste vs. Personal Hygiene

Kathryn couldn't understand why she had to practically throw her thirteen-year-old son into the shower. The teen guys at their church seemed to really care about their appearance, but it seemed Trent would go for days without showering if he could. Her husband, Hugh, offered some insight.

"Trent is a late bloomer," he said. "I was too. I remember feeling really self-conscious in gym class. I avoided showering like it was the plague. I would have rather had a root canal than shower with the other guys who had started maturing. That's probably how Trent is feeling."

"But I'm talking about showering at home," Kathryn said. "He's just not interested in being clean and looking his best. And yes, this bothers me!"

"Again, I think it's because he's a late bloomer. When he starts to mature physically, and when he becomes interested in girls, he'll shower at *least* once a day," Hugh said.

How would *you* handle this problem?

From Kathryn's viewpoint, it made sense to help her son understand that personal hygiene was a necessity. From Hugh's vantage point, his son was still just a boy—not yet a young man—and things would soon simply work out right when nature took its course.

Hugh and Kathryn compromised. Kathryn took Trent shopping for some trendy clothes and made an appointment with one of the best hair stylists in town. Because she let Trent select his clothes, he loved them. He also loved his new hairstyle and felt good about himself.

When they got home, Kathryn took photos of her son in his new clothes and sporting his new hairstyle and posted them on the fridge with the caption "Most Handsome Teen Guy in the World."

Though Trent complained about the pictures being in the kitchen, it actually made him feel pretty special. Later that evening, Kathryn announced the deal: "Trent, you look terrific! I know you love your new clothes, but you can only put them on *after* you've showered. And you can't wear them more than one time without tossing them into the dirty clothes bag."

Trent tried to bend the rules a few times, but Kathryn stuck to them and Hugh supported her. In less than a year, Trent began to mature, and as his dad had predicted, he was suddenly interested in personal hygiene.

He Doesn't Have to Be a Model

We're not saying your son has to look like he should be on the cover of a magazine, but *before* he reaches his teen years, you'll want to instill some good personal hygiene habits into his lifestyle. Showering often and having clean hair should be nonnegotiable.

But what about hairstyle? Ah. Here's where personal taste comes in. We encourage you to choose your battles carefully. As long as your son's choices don't involve a moral issue, give him some slack. He wants his hair a little longer than you prefer? If he's keeping it clean, let him try it.

He wants to highlight or completely change the color of his hair? Again, if he keeps it clean, don't make a battle out of this. What if he wants to *shave* his head? Though that may not be your preference, it's not a moral issue. You may cringe inwardly when he walks into church with a shaved head, but look on the bright side: He's in church! And his head is clean!

The same principle applies to clothing. As long as his clothes are clean and not suggestive (pants don't hang so low that his underwear is showing), let him experiment with a variety of styles. Betsy's son suddenly decided he loved the color black when he entered middle school. "We went shopping, and I had to force him to get a few shirts that were navy blue, brown, and gray," she said. "All he wanted was black clothing. I didn't know if he was just trying to look cool, or if he was going goth. But I hated to see him wear black so much."

Betsy finally told Jed that he could wear black three times a week to school and once a month to church. He didn't like it, but he obeyed. "Thankfully," she says, "it was just a phase. By the next year he was into boots and ropers. The next year it was the athletic look. I began to realize that he was just trying to find himself, and I'm glad I let him have some freedom to do so."

Again, if it's not a moral issue, decide that clothing and hairstyle aren't battles you need to fight. Save your time and energy for battles that involve moral issues.

Unplug the Media Wars

The latest shoot-'em-up, thrill-a-minute flick is exploding on the big screen, and your son can't wait to gobble up the action with his buddies.

"All my friends are going to see it," he says. "Can I go?"

"What's it rated?" you ask.

Suddenly lightning flashes behind you and ominous organ music fills the room. Then silence.

Your son swallows hard and nervously shifts his eyes. You can practically see the wheels spinning inside his head. *So what's his response this time? The usual?*

"Look," he says, "it has a few explosions, okay?" *Yep, it's the usual.*

"It's not PG and it's not suitable for little kids—I'll admit that," he continues. "But I'm not a little kid anymore. I can handle it, Mom."

You take a deep breath and fold your arms, bracing yourself for Media War No. 1,466,392.

Popular media—it's one of the biggest sources of conflict between parents and teenagers. We often get letters from teens that go something like this: "I wish my parents would ease up. After all, it's just a song/computer game/TV show/movie."

The fact is, we live in a mixed-up world of high-tech toys and low-tech values, and it's taking a toll on many families. Too many households—including Christian ones—have tuned in the voices of today's self-centered "greed-and-trash" culture, and have tuned out the ultimate truth—the Holy Word of God.

Like most parents, you're probably weary from the constant battles, but we urge you to hold your ground. Here are some suggestions:

Help Your Son Evaluate His Media Diet

The key is to help him know *why* being picky with media is important, know *what* to be picky about, then *take a stand* for what's right.

Use Philippians 4:8 as a guide to what's entering his eyes and ears: "Finally, brothers, whatever is true, whatever is noble, whatever is right, whatever is pure, whatever is lovely, whatever is admirable—if anything is excellent or praiseworthy—think about such things."

Encourage Him to Ask Hard Questions

- Is it true? Does this computer game mock what God says is good?

- Is it noble? Does this movie help me to develop a proper mind-set?

- Is it right? Is this TV program causing me to compromise biblical truths?

- Is it pure? Does this concert offer more treasure than trash to make it worth my time and money?

- Is it lovely? Would I be embarrassed if my youth leader found out I read this magazine?

- Is it admirable? Does this song offer wisdom and/or benefit me in any way?

- Is it excellent? Is this the best possible way for me to spend my time?

- Is it praiseworthy? Am I drawn closer to God because of it?

Tell Him That You Are What You Eat

Every song, book, video game, and movie has a philosophy. Some are into hedonism ("Get high, have sex, and party hearty!"). Others preach politics ("Kill the cops and overthrow the system!"). Still others promote pessimism and despair ("Life is meaningless!"). Obviously, the argument that "It's just harmless entertainment; it doesn't affect me" simply isn't true.

Stop the Violence: Switch Off Questionable Computer Games

Why do people make a big deal about certain interactive video games—claiming that some are too violent and even addictive?

After all, none of it is real, and players are totally in control. Right?—
Luke, 15

Face it: Guys love a good adrenaline rush. And for millions of boys in this country, the thrill of choice is just a click away. Yet can this form of entertainment actually be dangerous?

Lt. Col. David Grossman, director of the Killology Research Group, is an expert on what it takes to make soldiers more comfortable with taking another life on the battlefield. He sees a parallel with games that put players behind the eyes of the shooter. Just as a flight simulator teaches people to fly a plane, so point-and-shoot games can desensitize us and, in extreme cases, make people more efficient killers. Grossman offers some chilling observations:

In Paducah, Ky., a 14-year-old boy brought a .22 caliber pistol to school. He fired eight shots. For the sake of perspective, the FBI says that the average law enforcement officer hits less than one bullet in five in real-world engagement. This young man fired eight shots. He hit eight different students. And we know where he acquired this ability—from video games. His parents had converted a two-car garage into a playroom with VCRs and video games. He had become a master game player.

On that fateful morning, he acted out a set of conditioned responses. He walked in, planted his feet, posted the gun in a two-handed stance, and opened fire. He never moved far to the left or right. He just fired one shot at everything that popped up on his screen. A person's normal response is to shoot at a target until it drops, but video games train you to fire one shot and then move on. And so he proceeded. Most video games give bonus points for head shots. This young man hit five out of eight in that region.[1]

Okay, let's be reasonable. Few players will take gaming to that extreme, but the point is, a Christian young man shouldn't entertain himself with violence in the first place.

Author Diane Levin claims that surveys and studies prove kids in the United States average thirty-five hours each week playing computer and video games, as well as watching TV and movies.[2]

We urge you to steer him clear of violent computer games.

Not Just a Game

It's no secret that the U.S. military uses the video game Doom to teach soldiers how to kill. Some police officers use it too. And they're not just clowning around playing games on the job. Experts really believe that playing games like Doom helps policemen and soldiers learn how to kill in real life. How? Repetition is the key. Shooting their way through a violent video game over and over dulls their sensitivity to real-life killing.

Imagine the effects a violent computer game can have on an impressionable adolescent mind.

Despite the high-tech thrills and chills, too many video games pack a dangerous punch. But you can pull the plug on the bad stuff and help your son play smart.

Gaming Guidelines

Take a closer look. What kind of stuff is your son putting in his brain after school? Remember this: You can't trust Nintendo and Xbox to set your boy on the right path. That rating label on the box just doesn't cut it. Your best bet is to review a game before you buy it.

Help him to discern. The Bible tells us that we become what we see (Matthew 6:22). So if your son spends his time playing violent video games, what is he becoming? Help him understand that games such as Doom can desensitize him to sin. Tell him that just because it's on a computer or TV screen doesn't make it exempt from what God commands.

Restructure your son's gaming life. Ask your boy to think about how much time he spends tensed in front of a computer screen. How many hours is he attached to a video-game controller? Even if the game is relatively harmless, the *amount* of time devoted to it can take a toll on the balance of his life socially, spiritually, and mentally. The key: Create realistic guidelines, then hold him accountable to following through.

Keep in mind that not all computer and video games are bad. There are some great ones out there. It's just that certain games may make your son stumble in his Christian walk. Bottom line: Help your son avoid separating his game collection from his commitment to Christ.

Focus His Vision: School, Goals, and Beyond

Bart Simpson is the ultimate underachiever. He's content with average performance, his mind is focused on instant gratification, he doesn't count the cost of his actions, and he wastes energy concocting elaborate schemes for dodging responsibilities.

And when it comes to goals, his head is definitely in the ozone: "I'd like to be the first human to ever skateboard on Mars. Cowabunga, dude!"

Unmotivated. Unfocused. Unrealistic. Sound familiar? Unfortunately, Bart's world describes the planet occupied by too many teen guys.

Take seventeen-year-old Jason, for example. Since becoming a teen, Jason flunked out of school on more than one occasion, and he even got into some trouble with the law.

During a camping trip with his youth group, his pastor asked Jason, "What do you hope to accomplish during your lifetime?"

"I want to be a marine biologist," he responded, "or maybe a photographer."

"Great!" the pastor said. "Now, how do you think you can achieve these goals?"

"Humph!" Jason grunted as he shrugged his shoulders and poked a stick in the campfire. "I don't do too well at school, and I don't own a camera. I dunno. But each summer my mom takes me to Florida. I think snapping pictures or working with sea animals would be cool."

We're convinced that locked inside this boy is a future Jacques Cousteau or an Ansel Adams. Jason really is bursting with potential. The problem is, he lacks direction. Without the proper spark from his parents, he could end up wallowing in mediocrity—always dreaming, but never doing.

We're also convinced that the keys to motivating Jason (even Bart) center on these crucial steps:

Fuel his imagination. Get him excited about the future and all the possibilities ahead of him: the things he can experience, the places he can go, the man he can become. Encourage him to dream big and to explore a few possibilities right now. (This could mean taking photography lessons, volunteering at the local zoo, joining the band, or going out for a sport.)

Help him live beyond the moment. It's not unlike Jason to squander the present watching a *Godzilla* marathon on TV at the expense of tomorrow's big exam. Help your son realize that these kinds of irresponsible choices won't just result in bad grades, but they can also set in motion bad habits, behaviors that can end up stealing his dreams. Show him how today's choices can impact tomorrow's opportunities. Encourage him to begin setting realistic goals.

Build his self-esteem. We've met gang members in Chicago who would kill (or be killed) over a simple pickup basketball game. Why? They've anchored their lives to a game and have completely disconnected themselves from reality. To these boys, winning on the court equals self-worth. It's safe to say that your son wouldn't die over a basketball game, but perhaps he has been emotionally slammed on the court or in the classroom. Perhaps he's trapped in the lie that he'll never amount to much. Help him to see that his life is like a work of art that's still in process. Tell him that God would never say, "This is who you are—and who you'll always be." Instead, Jesus says, "Just imagine what you can become."

Break Bad Study Habits

As school rolls around each year, one thing usually happens for most teen guys: panic!

Homework assignments stack up, and term papers are put off until the last possible second. Cram sessions for tomorrow's big test become the norm. "Sleep?!" your teen says with a nervous twitch. "Uh—I'll catch up on that at Christmas . . . or maybe spring break!"

There is a better way. You can help your teen correct bad study habits, steer clear of the failure cycle, and get off on the right foot. "Homeschool" him in these GPA-boosting basics:

Teach him to tune in the teacher. If your son is constantly thinking about grand slam home runs and triple-decker burgers, he isn't getting what the teacher is saying. Three simple steps will maximize his classroom time.

- He must remind his brain to concentrate each time it wants to wander.
- Taking notes on what the teacher says, as well as on his reading assignments, will give him the edge he needs. Show him how to be an effective note-taker, and then encourage him to review them several consecutive nights before an upcoming test.
- Let him know it's okay to ask his teacher questions about the stuff he doesn't understand.

Teach him to stop procrastinating. What a concept! Yet most guys just don't seem to get this. They often have a hard time understanding that if their teachers assign fifteen pages of reading every night for a week, they must read a section *each night*. Chances are your son needs help getting organized and staying on track. Remind him that wise teens attack their homework on a daily basis so it won't end up attacking them.

Test insurance. Whether your son is dealing with a case of "test-taking jitters" or the fear of giving an oral report, remind him that God is nearby: "The Lord will keep you from all harm—he will watch over your life; the Lord will watch over your coming and going both now and forevermore" (Psalm 121:7–8).

CHAPTER 5

Making Contact:
Getting Through to Your Son

I fight a lot with my parents and younger sister, and I'm sick of it. When we argue, I try to understand their viewpoint. But 99 percent of the time they do not care what I have to say. Thus, they usually make decisions that are based on a tiny fraction of the facts, and that leads to irrational decision-making. I've tried to bring this up, but it never works because I'm quickly dismissed. And the only time we have peace is when I distance myself from them, because no contact usually means no fights. I don't know what to do.—Kevin, 15

My parents and I always fight no matter what it's about, and when I try to explain how I hate it when we fight, we end up fighting over fighting. I just don't know what to do!—Caleb, 15

Do you sometimes feel as though you're talking with an alien when you try to communicate with your son? Hopefully the emails above prove that teen guys *want* to have a good relationship with their family members; they *desire* good communication with you.

Opening Communication Lines

Here are three suggestions for improving communication with your son:

Whenever you drive your son somewhere, realize that you have a captive audience. So make an effort to be alone with him in the car as much as possible. This is a great time to gently probe (*gently* being the key word here) and find out what's going on inside his head.

Ask questions that require more than a yes/no answer. Establish "car time" as special time for the two of you. Here are a few examples to get started:

- What was the best thing about your day today?
- What was the worst thing about your day today?
- If you could have anything you want for dinner this weekend, what would it be? (Then try to make it for him.)
- What makes it most difficult to get along with your brothers and sisters?
- What do you wish were different about your relationship with your dad and me?

Be sensitive to specific times your son may be more apt to be open. And these will probably be the most inopportune times for *you.* He may be ready to unwind and finally talk about his day around midnight. If so, make time to sit on the edge of his bed and talk and pray with him.

You may want to start a dialogue with him as soon as he gets home from school, but your son may require some alone time first to simply unwind. If he needs to be alone in his room to deprogram, or if he needs to simply veg in front of the TV for half an hour, allow him that space.

Tune in to your son's communication style. Some guys just aren't that verbal. The key is finding a method of communication he's comfortable with and using that as an opening. Is your son a writer? Challenge him to complete a journal with you. Designate a specific notebook that you can pass between the two of you.

Begin with easy, fun, non-threatening statements and questions for your son to answer. Then have him make a list of questions for you to answer. As you get further along, deepen your conversations. If he's a poet or an artist, encourage him to include a poem or drawing as one of his answers. This is something you do at your own pace. Don't rush each other. It's not the time limit that's important; it's the process of communication that's valued. It's all about getting through to your son.

Your difficult-to-reach son may not be interested at all in journaling. What *is* he interested in? How does he best communicate? If he's a texting pro, start texting him! I have a friend who texts his sons during church. His son usually sits with friends, and Mark will text him fun little messages such as, "Did you catch what the pastor just said? Where else have you heard that? Dad's not such a dummy after all, huh?" Or, "Hey, champ! Wake up. It's almost time for lunch. Be ready to discuss sermon at Pizza Palace."

Your texts don't have to be long—just let your son know you're thinking about him and praying for him throughout his day. Texting can also be used to simply communicate the everyday happenings in your lives: "Dinner is going to be at five today. I'm making your favorite!"

If your son is a musician, challenge yourself to expose him to all kinds of music: jazz concerts in the park, the symphony, Christian concerts, secular concerts (within reason), classical, reggae, etc. Engage him in conversation about the music and lyrics. Ask him to write a song—funny or serious—about a recent experience.

Perhaps your son is into creating videos. Help him find places to connect and learn about the newest technology. Help him get started, and encourage him when he creates something. Help him discover how he can use his interests to glorify God. For example, could he put all the announcements for youth group (or church) on a short video? When he realizes you're supporting his hobby instead of tuning him out simply because it's not your personal interest, he'll be more apt to communicate with you more.

Is your son a DJ, an actor, an athlete? Again, discovering how he communicates—whether it's behind a mic, on the court, or on the stage—will help you get through to him. Take an active interest in every area of his life. Support him and strive to help him become the best he can be in these specific areas of expressing himself.

It's important to know, however, that communicating effectively with your son may change as *he* changes. The journal may be effective when he's thirteen but maybe not at seventeen. Or he may not be very interested in music at fourteen, but he may love it at sixteen. Let's look at a few different stages your son will experience and how that will affect your manner of connecting with him.

Ages 11 to 14

Your son is going through all kinds of emotional and physical changes during these years of adolescence. He may tend to get angry for no apparent reason. He may lash out at his younger sister. Remember that his hormones are waking up and basically going wacko!

Fourteen-year-old Kyle slams his bedroom door and won't eat supper because his college-aged sister said his feet are the size of skis. Last week he simply would've dished out a creative comeback, but now it's an entirely different matter.

Things that used to be fun are now seen as stupid. Instead of enjoying being with you, he's suddenly too busy to give you the time of day. But tomorrow may be totally different. How can you keep up without going crazy? Try to remember . . .

Your son lives in a world that demands he be a man. What *is* a man? According to the media, it's often someone who can get a girl into bed. Or it's the most masculine outdoorsman or an extreme sports athlete. Your son may try pushing some boundaries to achieve this status. He may attempt some daredevil stunts off the roof of your house he wouldn't have even considered a year ago. In short, he's not always thinking . . . let alone thinking clearly!

His friends are his lifelines to social acceptance. He'll want to spend more time with them than with you. This is totally normal. He may also spend a lot of time texting them. As he makes friends who are girls, he'll spend more and more time texting and talking on the phone.

He really does want you involved in his life but doesn't want you to tell him what to do. He's developing his independence and wants to make more of his own decisions.

He spends more time in his room behind closed doors. Chances are he's flexing his muscles, combing his hair differently, and playing video games. His own life is morphing right before his eyes.

He needs clear boundaries. His friends and the culture are telling him he should be independent and cutting ties with you, but he's not yet capable of making logical decisions on his own. His choices are more influenced by outside sources than ever before. He needs you to protect him from his own immaturity and inexperience.

Give him a little more freedom as he can handle it—in gradual stages. Keep close watch on who and what is influencing his choices.

He's beginning to notice girls. He's starting to get invited to boy-girl parties and may or may not be interested. If he *is* interested, he'll want attention from girls and may act inappropriately to get it.

He may be sarcastic. The friends he chooses to hang out with are a huge influence on how he acts, talks, and respects or disrespects you and others in authority. Know who his friends are. Don't be afraid to intervene if you see inappropriate choices in friends at this impressionable age. They are shaping who he's becoming—big time.

He's insecure with his body image. He may be getting hair in different places on his body, his voice is starting to change, and he needs your help in knowing he's normal. He may be developing earlier or later than his friends. This can be a confusing and even embarrassing time.

Help him through this awkward state. If his skin is breaking out, take him to a dermatologist or ask your pharmacist for over-the-counter treatments. If his crooked teeth are an embarrassment to him, bite the bullet and invest in braces.

Whatever you can do to help him feel comfortable in his own skin at this age is well worth the cost. This is a critical age for building self-confidence.

Rites of passage are important to him. Teens don't need much of a reason for a party. Make every accomplishment or milestone in his life a reason to celebrate. Give him goals to look forward to and work toward: trying out for the basketball team, making the honor roll, getting a part in the school play, completing his first track meet, committing to a purity pledge, and eventually shaving. All are cause for celebration. Life should be fun as you enter the teen years together!

Ages 15 to 16

This is a fun stage of your son's life. He's becoming more confident, and his talents and areas of interest are narrowing down. You're seeing him make more mature decisions and take on more responsibility.

He's wanting more money at this age. Darin was only fifteen, but he was starting to think ahead about getting a car. He gathered the things he wasn't using anymore such as clothing he'd outgrown and old toys and musical instruments and held his own garage sale. Though it didn't bring in enough money for a car, he had set the wheels in motion. He was encouraged enough at what he *did* make that he sought and found three part-time jobs throughout the summer and was able to keep one during the school year. When he turned sixteen, he had enough money to purchase a very, very used car. "We so admired his efforts," his dad, Greg, says, "that we decided to match what he had earned and saved. We're proud of the way he took ownership of needing to earn his own money."

At this age, guys are highly motivated to earn money. It may be a newspaper route, mowing lawns, or dog sitting, but allowing your son to get a part-time job will teach him a lot about handling cash and responsibility.

Your son is discovering what his talents are at this age. He'll become more involved in extracurricular activities at school or church and will keep you busy carpooling, at least until he gets that coveted driver's license! Support him in these activities. Attend his chess tournaments, his band concerts, his basketball games, or his karate meets.

His friends have become more of an integral part of his life. In fact, he's probably spending more time out of the house than in. Encourage him in the relationships he's building. Make your home available for him and his friends. Always have snacks ready for a hungry group of guys.

Riley's parents decided to finish their basement when their son turned fifteen because they wanted him to have a safe and fun environment where he could just hang with his friends. They got Riley and his friends involved in the decorating because they wanted him to take ownership of the basement.

Riley decided on a sports theme, and he and his buddies pooled their collection of Denver Bronco memorabilia. "We bought some navy blue leather couches and a flat-screen TV," his mom says, "but we left the decorating up to the boys. Broncos orange and blue pillows, rugs, and blankets adorn the room."

"It's really cool," Riley says. "It's sort of like a sports bar without the alcohol. We have a mini-fridge down there and we play Wii. It's great. My house is where everyone wants to be."

Your budget may not allow you to create a basement for your son and his friends, but you can still make your home a fun place to be. Always have your door open to his friends for after-the-game hangouts and pizza parties. Teens need safe places to congregate on weekends and after school.

Don't worry that your house isn't clean or big enough— they just want to be together. You can provide a warm and friendly environment right in your home for them to watch movies, play games, and raid your refrigerator. It doesn't take much—give them something to eat and you'll have the most popular house in town!

Your son sees himself becoming a man and is beginning to embrace his manhood. Even though the hormones are still raging, your son has become more comfortable in his body. You'll notice him working out more, wanting to join a health club, or jogging to enhance his physical stature.

Your son is discovering his individuality. So don't try to recreate another sibling. He may be completely different from his brother or sister. That's okay! Celebrate those differences instead of striving to make him into a carbon copy of your older son.

If he loves hiking, hike with him. If he enjoys writing, read his work and encourage him to develop his talent. If he's into drama, be his biggest cheerleader. If he enjoys tinkering with motors, help him find an auto mechanics class to join. Your son is one of a kind. Give him permission to be who he is wired by God to be.

He's starting to think about his future. Encourage him to seek God's plan for his life. It's a scary thing to try to figure out who he is and what he's made for with so many options out there to choose from. Guide him in discovering his talents and encourage him in those things.

He needs to know you have faith in him. Whether he makes the soccer team or gets a C on the test he was sure he failed, give your son the blessing of your faith in him. Maybe he had to take his driver's test twice before passing—make a big deal of his success rather than remind him that he failed it the first time.

Your son needs assurances from you, not sarcasm or teasing. Again, his body is still changing, and he's more sensitive to how he looks. Never joke about his hair, his growth (or lack of it), or his friends. I have a friend who used to tease his son as soon as he heard he liked a girl. "So you like Abby, huh? Have you sat by her yet? Held her hand? When are you going to do that? Huh?"

As soon as his dad started teasing him, the son shut down. Is it any wonder why the boy stopped talking to his dad about his personal life? He didn't want the hassle of being teased. Although his dad never meant to hurt him, he was unsure of how to communicate effectively with his son, so he simply resorted to something that felt comfortable: teasing and sarcasm. It cost them two years in their relationship.

Your role as a parent is changing too. Now's the time to step back *a little* and watch your young man become who he was uniquely created to be.

You can count on bumps to come if you continue to treat him as if he were eleven or twelve years old. In case you hadn't noticed, he's not a child anymore. Parenting needs to change when your son becomes a teenager. Threats of punishment for not making his bed or leaving a mess in the bathroom will go in one ear and out the other. He wants to be respected and talked to like he's an adult, not a child.

He still needs you—perhaps more than ever. He may experience his first date at this age and ask you for suggestions. Things may have smoothed out from the tumultuous middle-school years, or you may be in the heat of battle as the two of you get used to his being more independent and away from home so much.

Ages 17 to 19

At this age, Mom and Dad need to step back even more. Your son's out or nearly out of high school and on to college or a full-time job. He's now considered an adult by society and is taking more responsibility for himself and the consequences of his choices.

Your son needs your guidance now more than your lectures. If he gets a speeding ticket, he pays the fine. If he decides to go to college a thousand miles away from home, he'll live with the fact that he can't come home every other weekend. Connect with him by talking through these big decisions he's having to make. Show him the importance of handling responsibility (such as getting a speeding ticket) by how you model responsibility. Do you pay bills on time? Are you responsible to return the grocery cart to where it needs to go instead of leaving it in the parking lot? He's watching you, and the way he handles responsibility—big or small—will greatly depend on what he sees you model.

He wants you to talk *with* him, not *at* him. He wants your input but needs to make his own decisions. Be willing to *discuss* his choices instead of simply making the decision for him. For example, the curfew you have set for him is midnight, but he wants a two a.m. curfew. Instead of simply saying no, unpack the idea and discuss it with him.

"Restaurants are closed by midnight. What's there to do after midnight that's really worth doing?" Talk about it. It may be that he simply wants to be with his friends. "What will you and your friends do past midnight? Drive around? Pick up other friends? Go to someone's house? What kinds of trouble could you get into past midnight?" Help your son come to his own conclusion that a two a.m. curfew really isn't worth the hassle.

Dating and Relationships

In his later teen years, your son will thrive on opposite-sex relationships. Let's dive inside this topic for a few moments.

The very essence of manhood thrives on loving, being loved, and providing for himself and a family. How your son learns to do this has been largely influenced by what he has learned from you while watching your relationship with your spouse.

The best way to encourage your son to set his sights high in this important area of his personal life is by modeling a healthy and loving relationship with your husband:

- Do you respect your husband as a person, or are you using him to make you feel complete? Do you really want *him,* or do you simply want a man to take care of you?

- Are you interested in your hubby's thoughts, ideas, and preferences? What about in some of the everyday matters such as where you eat and what you do on weekends? Or does it appear to your son that you're only interested in what *you* want to do?

- Do you notice when your husband is sad, worried, or upset about something? Or does your son think you're self-centered?

- How do you represent your husband to your friends when he's not around? Do you complain about him or negate his worth?

- How do you treat your in-laws? Do you strive to visit them as much as your own side of the family? Do you honor and esteem them?

- Does your son see you bringing out the best in your husband and encouraging him to be all God wants him to be?

- Does your son notice that you allow your husband to treat you like a lady—opening doors for you, pulling out your chair before you sit down—or are you too independent and determined to do things your own way?

- Do you accept your husband as he is? Or do you try to get him to dress differently, style his hair another way, or drop his hobbies (golf, civic club, etc.) and only concentrate on you and your interests?

Assure your son of his precious worth and value as a man uniquely created by God. He should be careful about whom he gives his heart to and willing to wait for God's best in his dating life.

Again, understanding the different phases of life your son is going through will help you get through to him more effectively.

CHAPTER 6

Helping Him Unmask His "True Self"

Even though your son emulates the masculinity of his dad (or other men in his life), did you ever consider the role a mom plays in this process?

The fact is, you help shape your child's identity and transform him from boy to man in five key ways: (1) You teach him about the uniqueness of being *male* and *female*; (2) you show him how to relate appropriately with the opposite sex; (3) you polish his rough edges and train him in the finer points of "acting like a gentleman"; (4) you steer him clear of macho myths; (5) you nurture the courage he needs to unmask his true self.

I (Michael) never gave much thought to points 4 and 5 until my wife, Tiffany, filled me in on a lively conversation she had with two other moms.

Every day when school lets out for our eight-year-old son, Christopher, my wife and her two best friends—Katie and

Courtney (not their real names)—get together at a nearby park. As they watch their children burn off energy on the swings and the slides, the ladies swap stories or get on their soapboxes about current events. They even have Bible studies and prayer times. All three moms share the same views on parenting, faith, and politics, and they each have the unique challenge of raising boys.

Katie has three sons—ages eight, nine, and thirteen—and describes them as polar opposites of each other. Her eldest boy is quiet and has an aptitude for the arts, the middle child is easy-going and very social, and the youngest is a competitive thrill seeker. Courtney is busy with an imaginative nine-year-old novelist and a moody "tweenager" who is turning thirteen in a few months. Tiffany and I have one son—an energetic athlete who wants to be a veterinarian . . . or a NASCAR champion!

One day Katie scooted next to Courtney and Tiffany on a park bench and said, "Okay, I have a question: Is there some secret key to figuring out how a boy's mind works? I mean *really*, what in the world is going on up there?"

And with that, the three moms launched into a meaningful conversation about parenting—one that refined how they connect with their sons.

Here's how Tiffany recounted the dialogue to me. Like I said, it was a real eye-opener. Let's listen in:

Mom to Mom: How to Build a *Better* Boy

Katie: I'm seriously outnumbered by guys in my own home. There are days that I wonder if I'm losing my mind. It's like they are in their own world, and sometimes it just doesn't make any sense.

Courtney: It's all about "wrestle-ationships" in our house. When my husband and the boys aren't breaking the furniture—and each other—they're locked in to video games. The only normal conversations I have are with the two of you.

Tiffany: You mean conversations that don't end with someone getting angry or defensive? I'm trying to teach Christopher how to better handle his emotions, but I'm starting to lose it. It's as if Christopher is on an emotional roller coaster, and he's not even a teenager yet. His entire way of processing is completely different from mine. It's exhausting!

Courtney: I know! It's like every time I think I have it figured out, it changes.

Katie: It's a mystery, but it definitely reveals how amazing God is. I mean, He made us in His image—male and female. We are wired so differently. And yet it works best when we have each other.

Courtney: Yet all of this must be so confusing for boys, you know? I remember how hard it was, trying to figure out who I was at that age. And I didn't have to sort through half the stuff these guys deal with. There are so many expectations put on males: *Boys are supposed to act like this, look like that, play these sports, hang out on these Web sites, and have girlfriends.* It's like they are being overloaded with so many people trying to tell them *who* they are supposed to be.

Tiffany: I know. It's like they have to figure out twice as much stuff as we did at their age. Males seem to have a Guy Code that they conform to.

Katie: I've always thought my kids would come to me for advice. But I'm already seeing my older boys withdraw when they get stressed. I have to find a way to let them know that what they are going through is normal—and survivable. I don't want them to be brainwashed by the Guy Code.

Courtney: I am so glad to know I'm not the only one going through this. So what do we do?

Katie: I guess we just stay steady. I mean, their hormones are bouncing all over the place. We have to be the sane ones, right?

Tiffany: It's so hard. Stay steady and pray a lot.

Courtney: It's so hard when parenting becomes a partnership with your kid. I know that I have to keep leading, but it seems that *supporting* my kids is becoming more and more important. I need to find new ways to let them know they can count on me when they get overwhelmed and confused.

Tiffany: Even support all of their crazy boy ways?

Courtney: Boys are wired to be boys. I guess the trick is to teach them how to be men. We can never, ever make the mistake of turning a boy into a girl. God gave them all of the testosterone—who am I to try to change that? Anyway, I can always have nice furniture once they are all off to college.

Katie: Look, it's up to our husbands to model masculinity. But it's our job to smooth out the rough edges. We teach our sons to be gentlemen. And we help them unmask their true selves. That's my goal as a mom.

Can you relate to these moms? Do you agree with their observations? How about the warning from Courtney ("Never, ever make the mistake of turning a boy into a girl.")? As you help your son polish his rough edges, we encourage you to celebrate his gender, guide him toward authentic masculinity, and help him to be comfortable with the unique person God created him to be.

Why Sane Guys Do Crazy Things

It all comes down to hormones coupled with the way males develop neurologically. In a very real sense boys have been wired by God to be risk takers, which is why, as Dr. James Dobson points out in his book *Bringing Up Boys*, "One of the scariest aspects of raising boys is their tendency to risk life and limb for no good reason." Dr. Dobson cites a study that compares the risk-taking behaviors of boys and girls, concluding that females usually weigh the consequences and "are less likely to plunge ahead if there is any potential for injury."[1]

Many guys, on the other hand, focus on the thrill of the moment, not the big picture. They'd rather impress their friends and prove their manhood than look weak. And as Katie, Courtney, and Tiffany discovered in the opening dialogue, boys are under pressure. Early in life they are told, "Don't flinch," "Avoid looking weak," "Never cry," "Just suck it up and be a man." Consequently, they mistakenly believe that measuring up means following a rigid Guy Code. Add a boy's sense of invulnerability—the feeling that "I won't get hurt"—and you've got a potentially dangerous mix.

Meet Jeff, Brian, and Shane, three real teens who ended up getting snared in some common macho traps:

Macho Trap No. 1: Letting the Crowd Rule

Sun. Sand. Surf. A perfect stretch of a Florida beach is exactly what Jeff had in mind for spring break. So why was he sitting in the back of a police car instead of having a good time?

"The guys and I got caught hanging from a hotel balcony," the eighteen-year-old says later. "I should have said no when they handed me another beer—and a stupid dare. But everyone was cheering, and I felt as if my manhood was on the line. A guy faces a lot of pressure to act macho. How'd we get so messed up?"

Macho Trap No. 2: Sex on the Brain

It was a sticky summer night in Lake Charles, Louisiana, but sixteen-year-old Brian wasn't complaining. He was reclining on the sun porch of his parents' house—with his arms wrapped tightly around the waist of a girl he had met a few days earlier.

His folks' weekly date night provided an ideal opportunity for some romance of his own. Brian promised himself he wouldn't go all the way, since he'd made a pledge for purity at church.

But everything else . . .

We're not doing anything wrong, he tried to convince himself. *Besides, I have zero experience. It's time to grow up and be a man.*

Macho Trap No. 3: Believing He Is Invincible

Shane, age twenty, was a college football player with a promising future. Now he sits in a wheelchair. On a dare, Shane had tried to smash open a steel door—helmet first. Smoking marijuana at the time didn't help.

"I can't quite figure out why I did it," he says. "I know doing drugs was a factor. But whenever I get with the guys, it's like something else takes over. I feel invincible. I feel charged. And if I don't step up and prove myself, I don't feel like much of a man."

Is Your Son at Risk?

Smart guys, stupid choices, right? Yet these are more than just snapshots of testosterone-driven males overdosing on a good time. The boys in these stories illustrate the macho misconceptions that trap so many males today—otherwise known as the Guy Code.

Cultural Stereotypes. For Jeff, cultural stereotypes play a big part in defining manhood. To him, a true man looks, talks, and behaves by a crowd-approved standard. Yet he made a hopeful observation: "How'd we get so messed up?"

Sexual Intercourse. Brian thinks that being a man boils down to having sex. He's torn by his convictions, so he decides to push the limits. Eventually, though, he gives in to the heat of the moment. "It's crazy," he says. "I got what I wanted, yet I still don't feel like a man."

Brute Strength. Shane was convinced that real men conquer the competition and prove themselves through brute strength. Being confined to a wheelchair is a devastating new reality. Today, he's rethinking everything he once believed about life, truth, and his own journey into manhood.

Where is your son in the process? How does he define manhood? In his opinion, at what point does a boy become a man? And once a guy gets there, how does he know if he measures up?

Chances are your son feels very confused about what "real masculinity" means. After all, you and the church tell him one thing, friends say something different, and the media often paints a picture that's impossible to live up to.

Take a look at what guys are telling us. . . .

It's as if guys are expected to be macho clones, and I'm sick of it. At school, I have to put on this stupid tough-guy armor and be who the crowd says I should be. I wish I could just be myself. If I'm not the bully, I become the bullied.—Brad, 16

The world of teen guys can be a scary jungle. If we show any kind of weakness, we're hunted down and destroyed by "alpha" males. Tough guys prey on the weak.—Weston, 15

You'd think guys in the church would be different—but often they aren't. Even Christian males are scared inside. We put on acts and copy the world. I want to be different! I want to start being the man God created me to be.—Shane, 17

I don't feel like I fit in anywhere. I look in the mirror, and I don't even know who I am. I look around school, even my youth group, and all I see are cliques and clones. The so-called "cool kids" only hang out with other "cool clones." And if you don't measure up, life is cruel.—Devon, 16

Sometimes I feel lost, lonely, and forgotten. At other times, I feel as if every eye is on me—like I'm the featured act in today's teenage freak show!—Ian, 15

Teen guys are so messed up. I know because I am one. If you don't look, talk, and act a certain way, you're constantly picked on. Life is hell for guys—and parents and teachers are clueless.—Steven, 14

Male Myth Busters

Despite all the confusion, it's your job to help your son figure out how to be a godly guy—and avoid the traps that can strain relationships, block spiritual growth, and lead to lifelong regrets.

How? Challenge him to examine the most popular myths and compare them to what the Bible says about authentic manhood.

In reality, tough guys aren't afraid to show emotion. They've even been known to shed a tear during movies, kiss babies, and pick flowers for someone they like. Moms must drive home the truth that manhood isn't grounded on brute strength, athletic ability, or "female conquests." Instead, a man shows his strength by having the courage to be different. He walks with honor, stands strong with integrity, pursues purity in word and deed . . . and loves God with all his heart, mind, and soul.

"Manhood = Macho"

Myth: A real man is rough, tough, crude, cold, hard, harsh, silent, stone-faced, emotionless, and passionless. He never sheds a tear and always wears a poker face.

Truth: "Be on your guard; stand firm in the faith; be men of courage; be strong" (1 Corinthians 16:13).

A godly guy redefines *macho*. While he isn't always nice, he tries to be *good*.

- He's a protector, a servant, a soul-keeper, a lover, and a leader.
- He is a poet-warrior: The masculine soul is sometimes gritty and untamed, sometimes refined and gentle.
- He confidently expresses his emotions and draws true strength from the One who sets the standard for manhood: Jesus Christ.

Mom to the rescue: Point your son to Jesus' life as his best example of manhood. Jesus was caring, protective, and bold. He was the son of God, but served others with love. He sets a high standard, the best one we have. He was completely man. He grew up as a young Jewish boy, a carpenter's son who was anxious to take on his role as a man. He debated his elder scholars in the temple at an early age. Yet he went out of his way to love every child he met.

While your son is not always going to get it right, that's okay. Encourage him to take his confusion directly to Christ himself. Every mistake will make him stronger. A life of prayer will keep him focused during this time of craziness.

"'Man Funk' Is the Scent of True Masculinity"

Myth: Clean underwear?! What's that? Sensitivity, showering, shopping—that's girly stuff! Men are too busy fixing cars, watching sports on TV, drinking beer, belching, scratching, and telling dirty jokes.

Truth: "So God created man in his own image, in the image of God he created him; male and female he created them" (Genesis 1:27).

A godly guy doesn't conform to cultural stereotypes of masculinity or allow the crowd to tell him who he should be.

- He draws confidence from the fact that he is in every sense a *real man* because that's how God designed him.
- He is distinctly masculine, which makes him distinctly different from a woman—and unique from every other human on earth.
- He was created for a divine purpose. God's call upon his life perfectly matches his identity.

Mom to the rescue: Now might be a good time to go down memory lane. A mom's stories of her own teen years might come in handy here. While your son may not want to hear them, try anyway. They just might speak volumes. Tell him your memories of how the boys you knew were all busy trying to impress each other. Tell him how you were always looking for the one who stood out and had the confidence to be himself. Explain that even if it doesn't seem possible, having the courage to make his own path proves he is far more mature than all of the other clone-like boys.

"Having Sex Is the Mark of Manhood"

Myth: The ability to make sperm, ejaculate, and have sexual intercourse is what separates the men from the boys.

And first-time sex is a guy's initiation into the brotherhood of men.

Truth: "It is God's will that you should be sanctified: that you should avoid sexual immorality; that each of you should learn to control his own body in a way that is holy and honorable, not in passionate lust like the heathen, who do not know God" (1 Thessalonians 4:3–5).

A godly guy knows that engaging in sex doesn't transform a boy into a man. A person's sexuality is part of *who he is*—this is how God created us: male and female!

- He realizes that his sexuality is good and that he must honor his Creator with this sacred part of his life.
- He's convinced that sexual intercourse can be fun, thrilling, and passionate when used right (within the bonds of holy matrimony).
- He knows it can be unsatisfying, painful, cruel, and dangerous when misused (casually through premarital sex).

Mom to the rescue: A mom should never laugh or think her son's feelings for the opposite sex are silly or childish. His hormones are running crazy, and his feelings are very real. If you don't take them seriously, he will just think you don't understand. It will give him one more reason to withdraw into his silence. Remember, he is still part child and he lives in the moment. He doesn't have the life experience to see twenty years down the road—the here and now *is* his life. It's your job to stay steady and guide him. Ask him a lot of questions, and then *listen* to what he is trying to tell you. Don't be overwhelmed. Now is the time to be the adult.

"A Man Lives in the Moment"

Myth: Life is short and then you disappear. Who cares about anything that comes after that?

Truth: "Man is destined to die once, and after that to face judgment" (Hebrews 9:27).

A godly guy takes responsibility for his actions.

- He knows his choices have consequences, so he makes an effort to (1) count the cost and (2) make the most of every opportunity.

- He believes his reputation speaks loudly about his character.

Mom to the rescue: Never belittle his desire to prove himself. At the same time, don't make too much of it either. It's important to understand his need to break free and find himself, but he is just a teen. Ask him some questions: *Do you think your everyday decisions affect the rest of your life? Which decisions are long lasting? Why? Which ones are no big deal? Why? Do you worry about how your friends will react to your decisions? Do you ever give advice to your friends? Are your actions going to help you achieve your life goals? What are your life goals? Do you think it is possible to learn from someone else's stupid decisions? Like what?* Help him to train himself to ask these questions. Stepping back and considering the consequences is a lifelong discipline that will help him live a life of discernment.

"A Real Man Never Takes Off His Armor"

Myth: A man is "the strong silent type," never fully letting anyone into his heart.

Truth: "If I speak in the tongues of men and of angels, but have not love, I am only a resounding gong or a clanging cymbal. If I have the gift of prophecy and can fathom all mysteries and all knowledge, and if I have a faith that can move mountains, but have not love, I am nothing" (1 Corinthians 13:1–2).

A godly guy loves the way Jesus loves.

- He believes that love is sacrificial, serving, giving—and involves laying down his life for someone else.
- He knows God created men to be relational, despite what our culture tells us.
- He strives to love and to be loved.

Mom to the rescue: Encourage your son to get his eyes off himself and to start being a hero to others. Get him to think about all the different ways he can be Christ's hands and feet in the lives of others. Challenge him to do one of these things: make food for someone, visit people in a nursing home, help a friend clean his room or do homework, buy a meal for a homeless person, invite a friend to youth group, buy a friend a CD (even if it isn't his or her birthday), or take neighborhood kids to a baseball game. The idea is to do the unthinkable, something someone might never expect.

"Manhood Is All About Survival of the Fittest"

Myth: Real men are athletic, ruthless, and wired for one thing: crushing the competition through brute strength.

Truth: "To the weak I became weak, to win the weak. I have become all things to all men so that by all possible means I might save some. I do all this for the sake of the gospel, that I may share in its blessings. Do you not know that in a race all the runners run, but only one gets the prize? Run in such a way as to get the prize. Everyone who competes in the games goes into strict training. They do it to get a crown that will not last; but we do it to get a crown that will last forever. Therefore I do not run like a man running aimlessly; I do not fight like a man beating the air" (1 Corinthians 9:22–26).

A godly guy has a healthy perspective on competition.

- He knows that the Lord isn't impressed with shiny trophies and first-place awards. God looks at other stuff: hearts transformed by His power, eyes focused on His will, hands involved in His service.

- He doesn't turn every game into a contest that proves who's superior. Instead, he switches his goal from "clobbering the competition" to making a good shot, executing a good pass, playing by the rules, improving his skills, and setting the right example.

Mom to the rescue: Help your son control his compulsion to compete and maintain a healthy balance. Encourage him to run down this checklist:

☐ I'll remember that competition is temporary—as with everything in this world. But God's kingdom lasts forever. I'll keep my focus on His values and His will for my life.

☐ I'll never buy the lie that winners are only those who excel. My worth as an individual is based on who God says I am—His kid—not on how well I do.

☐ I'm committed to drawing my strength from God—especially during competition. I'll ask Him to change my desires and attitudes. I'll ask Him to teach me to put the fun back in the game.

☐ I'll keep in mind that 1 John 5:11–12 is the only yardstick to measure true winners and losers in life: "And this is the testimony: God has given us eternal life, and this life is in his Son. He who has the Son has life; he who does not have the Son of God does not have life."

CHAPTER 7

Lust, Sex, and Dating

You're probably well aware that a teen boy's appetite for sex can often seem like an inner tornado. In fact, there are four sexual storms that strike most young men (often with intense magnitude): lustful fantasy, masturbation, pornography, and the temptation to be sexually promiscuous.

It's important that your son gain self-discipline in each of these areas. God commands it, and girls and women deserve it. When we sat down to write these words, we counted literally thousands of emails from guys and their families on just about every sexual issue you can think of. Many boys felt defeated by lust, and their parents were clueless about how to help. In these actual letters, we're choosing to address a guy's questions with *you* in mind. In other words, our goal is to provide you with the advice you'll want when needing to answer a question similar to these. We think you'll find at least one question that will relate to your son, and we hope our answers will give you insight on how to guide him.

Lust Control = Thought Patrol

I've struggled with pornography since I was twelve. I hate what lust does to my relationship with Christ. What I do makes me sick, but when temptation presents itself, it seems so attractive. I talk to my dad all the time about my struggles, and he's very supportive and forgiving. Yet I can't seem to avoid surfing the Internet or fantasizing about sex. After I've lusted, I feel horrible. I promise God that it won't happen again. Then a few days later, I end up doing the same things. I feel like the apostle Paul: "For what I want to do I do not do, but what I hate I do" (Romans 7:15). I want freedom from lust. I feel as if I'm in a big hole, and I keep digging in deeper. Can you help me out?—Kyle, 17

I can't take back control over my mind. Thoughts about sex enter my head all the time. I know that it's a God-given thing to have a desire for sex. Yet I feel so guilty about the stuff in my brain. I'm sick of living this way. I want help. I want change!—Russ, 15

I'm a young man who is preparing for a career in Christian ministry, yet I still act like a child and play around with sexual temptation: I look at pornography, I masturbate constantly, and I treat women like objects instead of the amazing people God created them to be. I feel pathetic and ashamed. I'm ready to get my life right. Where do I start?—Sean, 19

I'm really going out on a limb with this. I've been dealing with lust for several years now, and it really seems like I'm in a losing battle. I can make commitments to stay pure, and I can even manage to keep them for a while, but I always seem to fall back into sin. I'm tired of keeping it a secret. I feel that God is calling me to establish accountability somehow with someone. What should I do next?—Matt, 17

Boys like Kyle, Russ, Sean, and Matt are struggling and desperately want a plan that will help them defeat lust. (Chances are, your son can relate.) The first step for every young man is getting to a place of total honesty—with themselves, with their parents, and especially with God. They must have the courage to admit their weaknesses and say "ENOUGH!" They simply cannot allow sin to have footholds in their hearts. But in order to get to this point, they must understand what they are dealing with.

That's where you can help.

Every mom and dad should communicate three things about this universal battle:

Lust must be "fed" to survive. Prolonged sexual thoughts and desires can't exist without anyone's permission. We simply cannot allow our minds (and our eyes) to feast on things that fuel those desires. Help your son to steer clear of known fantasy feeders: provocative movies, songs, magazines, Web sites. Help him realize that he has enough sexual temptation without stirring up more on purpose.

Lust is the opposite of love. The desire to be close to someone special is a natural God-given desire. Satan has perverted that desire, trying to convince us that the opposite sex was created to fulfill a sexual fantasy. Therefore, a boy may think he wants sex, but what he really wants is a friend he can share his life with one day in marriage. Help him to never settle for a cheap thrill when he can save himself for true intimacy in marriage.

Lust will beat your son if he plays one-on-one. But it can't beat his "team." Who's on your son's team? Several players: the Holy Spirit (He can give your son the power to overcome sin—when he asks), God's Word (God can show him verses to use as an offensive weapon against impure thoughts), his pastor, a close Christian guy friend, and especially his dad. Let your son know that most guys on his team have faced (or are facing) the same struggle.

Help Him Understand What's Happening

Sexual arousal starts in the mind—sometimes subconsciously—and the nervous system triggers his body to respond, complete with increased heart rate and an erect penis.

That means the key to counterattacking lust is to filter what he takes into his brain. What connects his brain to the rest of the world? His senses. And for your son, probably the most important sexual sense is sight. It's the way God wired guys: They're turned on visually. This is why pornography is such a huge industry and such a stumbling block even to committed Christian guys. One little glance, one quick peek and—*wham*—it's sex on the brain for most guys.

So what can your son do? Here are some steps he must take in order to head off lust:

Be prepared. There are two types of turn-on tempters: the ones he can avoid and the ones he can't. Your son can't do anything about the girl passing him on the street, but he can avoid the dark places on the Internet and TV. Explain that temptation is always just around the corner. Encourage him to keep his guard up.

Stay busy. King David was kicking back on the palace roof instead of being in battle with his men when he took his sexual fall (2 Samuel 11). Lounging all the time is an open invitation to fill the boredom with lust.

Monitor who he spends time with. His friends' language, habits, attitudes, and humor will have a significant impact on him.

How Moms Can Effect Change

Rest assured, your son is moving in the right direction if he senses that something's wrong inside and he desires change. If your boy has admitted his own battle with lust, it probably means that God is working on his heart, pointing out behaviors that He will cleanse and heal. Your son must allow the Holy Spirit to continue this work in him. Tell him to get alone and to have an honest, heart-to-heart conversation with Jesus.

At this point, it's important that your husband (or other trusted adult male) steps up and shows your son how to bring his sexual struggles into the light. No doubt your teen will feel shame and embarrassment, and he will prefer to hide from the issues he's dealing with. But tell him this: "God already knows what you think and do in private, and He understands your struggles better than you. Pray and confess your sins and weaknesses to Him. Acknowledge before Him your lack of power to control your sexual urges."

Next, pray daily for your son. Ask God to heal your son's sexuality, making it the wonderful thing He intends it to be. Encourage his dad to pray these things *with* your teen.

The key to healthy sexuality is outlined in Scripture. Here's what the apostle Paul wrote in 1 Thessalonians 4:3–5: "It is God's will that you should be sanctified: that you should avoid sexual immorality; that each of you should learn to control his

WHAT YOUR SON ISN'T TELLING YOU

own body in a way that is holy and honorable, not in passionate lust like the heathen, who do not know God." Share this passage with your son.

There's one last step you must help your son take—and it could be the hardest one of all: Make sure he meets regularly with an accountability partner (preferably his dad). He must confess his struggles to a trusted, older male role model weekly, if not daily. Guys need other guys in the battle to defeat sexual temptation.

Remind your son that we all have to account for our choices in life. This reality actually terrified Paul and motivated him to strive to please God in everything he did (see 2 Corinthians 5:9–11). Christian author Henry Blackaby has also wrestled with this issue. In his book *Experiencing God Day by Day,* here's what he concludes: "God does not force His will upon us. He will ask us to answer for the way we responded to Him. Christians have been pardoned by the sacrifice of Jesus. We are not condemned. But because God is absolutely just, we will be called on to give an account of our actions."[1]

Bottom line: With God's help, every guy must seek self-control over his sexuality. Our Lord requires it, girls have a right to it, and, above all, it enables him to develop into the godly man he was created to be.

An Appetite for Sex

I think about sex all the time, and I occasionally look at porn. Almost every day I read stories that contain sexually explicit material just so I can get pleasure from it. I always have fantasies about having sex, and I think it's becoming a problem. I don't know what to do or who I should talk to. Am I weird? Am I a sex addict?—Ben, 14

If two unmarried people are having sex in a committed relationship, what should stop them? As a Christian, I've always been taught that premarital sex is wrong, but the problem is, I can't find Scripture that says this specifically. Why do Christians create so many rules for something that everybody is doing?—Alex, 17

I totally agree that pornography is wrong. I am very curious about where the Bible draws the line between what's good and what's considered to be sexual sin. I was wondering if masturbation is a sinful act. There are several references in the Bible that tell us not to lust, which is synonymous with fantasizing. However, God does not condemn sex, and actually uses it as a way for married couples to bond. For that matter, are sexual mental images sinful before marriage? How about after marriage?—D. Wong, 15

How do you know if you've lost your virginity? I'm a Christian, and my girlfriend and I fell into temptation. We groped each other once. We both realize that what we did was wrong, but now we're afraid that we lost our virginity. Am I missing something? Does sex involve more than intercourse?—Dan, 16

Film critic Roger Ebert once noted, "It used to be that teenagers would go to the movies to see adults having sex. Now adults go to the movies to see teenagers having sex."[2]

Sadly, his observation is all too true. Step into a theater, click on the TV, or surf the Web and you can't help but wonder if morality has gone the way of the dinosaur. And all this can lead your son to believe that sexual purity is just plain weird—even for Christians!

WHAT YOUR SON ISN'T TELLING YOU

Despite our mixed-up sexual climate, your son needs to hear the truth: God created sex to be experienced between a husband and a wife in marriage. Anything apart from His awesome design is apart from His will. "Do not be deceived: Neither the sexually immoral nor idolaters nor adulterers nor male prostitutes nor homosexual offenders nor thieves nor the greedy nor drunkards nor slanderers nor swindlers will inherit the kingdom of God" (1 Corinthians 6:9b–10).

Moms, understand this: Most young men feel alone in their struggles and ashamed of their sexual desires. That's why you and your husband must communicate these two facts: (1) "You're normal!" (2) "Your appetite for sex truly is a good, healthy, God-given thing! The Lord doesn't want you to turn off these desires (as if you could). Instead, He wants to help you control them."

Lead Him to the Truth

Maybe it's time you and your son did a little research on the computer. *Not* everybody is "doing it." And if he believes they are, he's living in a fantasy world! Help him realize that the media *wants* him to believe everyone's doing it. And they've gone overboard to make teens feel that if they're *not* doing it, they're abnormal. But who cares what the media says? God has a much higher calling on our lives!

Share something like this with your son: "Here's the problem. God created sex as a beautiful union to glue two people together forever. So think of sex as a bonding agent, an extremely strong glue. Once you've had sex with someone, the two of you are glued together closer than any two people can become. It's just stupid to be glued to someone you're not married to. If you seriously want to be bonded to this person forever, then marry her right now and enjoy a life of intimate bonding the rest of your lives."

The Bible actually has a lot to say about sex. We don't have room to list everything here, but we think this Scripture is pretty strong: "Marriage should be honored by all, and the marriage bed kept pure, for God will judge the adulterer and all the sexually immoral" (Hebrews 13:4).

Does your son want to be all that God desires him to be? If he desires a lifetime of exciting sex, he must understand that waiting is the key. God wants to give him this amazing gift. Instead of going into marriage with regrets, he must wait. He must hold out for God's very best!

How Moms Can Promote Purity

Begin by letting your son know how much you appreciate his honesty. While it's understandable to be wary if he is expressing concerns echoed in some of the emails above, know that your son's curiosity is normal. Of course, it would be more comforting if his heart reflected that of D. Wong: "I am very curious about where the Bible draws the line between what's good and what's considered to be sexual sin."

What steps should *you* take in order to help your son establish biblical standards for sex? Try this:

First, encourage your teen to talk with his father. If he doesn't have a Christian dad in the home, let him know he can always talk with you, his mom. Make every effort to not act disgusted or shocked, but let him know you care enough to get him the help he needs. Explain that you want to make an appointment for him with a professional Christian counselor.

Remind your son that he can always talk with Christ. Pray with him. Let him know that Jesus understands what he's battling, because He faced temptation too. Thankfully, Christ can give your son the power to keep from giving in.

Here's a great verse for the two of you to memorize together:

> But remember this—the wrong desires that come into your life aren't anything new and different. Many others have faced exactly the same problems before you. And no temptation is irresistible. You can trust God to keep the temptation from becoming so strong that you can't stand up against it, for he has promised this and will do what he says. He will show you how to escape temptation's power so that you can bear up patiently against it. (1 Corinthians 10:13 TLB)

But What If My Son Has Gone Too Far?

Let him know that the guilt he may be feeling isn't all bad. It proves he has a tender conscience. God can work through a tender heart and mind, and He wants to forgive him for what he and his girlfriend have done. Pray with him, and encourage him to seek God's forgiveness. Then begin a discussion on helping him establish boundaries for his dating relationships. He may even need to list them on paper so the two of you can discuss them. Suggest he allow a spiritually mature adult to hold him accountable to those boundaries.

Though it will be uncomfortable, be willing to answer his questions on sex. *Intercourse* occurs when the male's penis penetrates the female's vagina. But the medical definition of sex is any contact with someone else's genitals.

Here are two messages you can communicate that will help to get him back on a righteous walk.

"You're not alone." The silence of sexual struggles has pushed too many Christian guys over the edge. And young men end up keeping quiet about their "deepest, darkest sins" because they buy a lie: "If I say something, I'll be condemned by everyone— my church, my parents, even God." Make sure the teen in your life understands that he is not alone in his failures—and that he doesn't have to be alone in his healing.

"God knows—and forgives." Chances are, your son has tried to hide his sins for a long time. Maybe he has confessed them to God yet is still entangled in guilt, flogging himself for his mistakes. Let him know that he is forgiven by God—and by you. Here's what he desperately needs to hear from his parents: "God knows your deepest secrets and sins—and He loves you despite them! You're not condemned for what you've done. If you confess your sin and repent, Jesus Christ forgives you and doesn't hold it against you. And that goes for us as well. We love you, we support you, and we are here for you. Together with God, we will help you overcome this struggle."

We can't say it enough: Stress that God wants to forgive him. But explain to your son that the true meaning of repentance means he'll turn around and go the opposite direction. So what does that mean for him? Hopefully he'll see (with your guidance) that it means no more time alone with simply him and his girlfriend. Tell him to stay in the light! Stay with other people! Do things with friends! With God's help, he can turn around and live a life of sexual purity.

Masturbation: Every Guy's Battle?

> I feel like I'm addicted to masturbation, and I'm totally out of control. I don't look at porn anymore—me and my friends got together with our dads and took out that battle! Yet masturbation is still a struggle. How do I overcome it? I'm going through a stressful time in my life, and it almost seems to help me relax. But I feel that masturbation is not right. What should I do?—Isaiah, 15

> I play on the varsity soccer team at my school. After practices sometimes the coach tells us to hit the showers. Well, most of the guys masturbate in the shower room, and they tried to get me to join them. I did it one time, but I felt guilty later. Is it a sin to masturbate?—Josh, 16

> I have a problem: I need to "un-master" masturbation. I do it somewhat often: Four to five times a week. Most of the time I don't want to do it. But it has become a habit. I need to know how to stop. Is it common for other teens to masturbate this much? HELP!—B.J., 16

Every guy struggles with something.

Maybe it's lust. Maybe it's porn. *Maybe it's masturbation.* Regardless of the battle, he's sick of faking it.

His stomach turns every time he knows he crosses a line, but still walks into church with a Walmart smile—acting as if he has it all together. *If others knew the real me,* he thinks, *I'd be the loneliest guy on earth.*

The guys we've talked to are ready to end the double life. They yearn to tear off the mask and become the authentic, one-of-a-kind man God has created them to be. They're tired of being defeated by lust, porn, and masturbation.

Chances are, your son feels the same way, and he needs your help.

How Moms Can Start a Healthy Dialogue

It begins by answering this question: Where do you and your husband stand on the issue of masturbation? Do you believe that abstaining is the best approach? Or do you view it as a harmless way of releasing sexual pressure?

Could it be that the two of you are somewhere in the middle? Or maybe you don't have an opinion at all. Perhaps you're uncomfortable even mentioning the M word. And the truth is, your son might not be quite comfortable doing it, yet he feels as if it's next to impossible to stop.

So what's a family to do? And how can a parent help? Even though boys aren't alone in their battles with masturbation, why are so many churches silent about it? Why do so many Christians feel confused about this issue?

Despite our culture's preoccupation with sex, our sexuality and sexual development are very private, personal matters. And historically, there have been a lot of myths and scary facts floating around, or even being taught, about masturbation. But maybe the biggest silencer is guilt. Satan loves to heap it on, and he'd love to use it to drive a wedge between you and God.

As you probably already know, when masturbation becomes a habit for your son, it brings with it feelings of guilt and shame. Are these feelings from God? Does this mean that regular masturbation is sin?

This whole subject would be much easier to deal with if there were a Bible verse that said, "Thou shalt not," or "Verily, it is okay." But the Bible is absolutely silent on this issue. While there are those who claim Genesis 38:8–11 condemns

Onan for masturbation and that 1 Corinthians 6:9–10 refers to this habit, the Bible scholars we've talked with believe these arguments are taken completely out of context.

We certainly don't want to contradict what you and your church believe. But we hope you'll carefully weigh the insights, Scriptures, and opinions presented in this section.

What Your Son Needs to Hear

"Don't think of yourself as weird." He must understand that many other Christian guys struggle with this too. So he doesn't have to feel strange for having a desire to masturbate. Also, if he doesn't struggle—tell him that there's nothing wrong with that either.

"Gain the right perspective." Considering that masturbation is unmentioned in the Bible, we can only conclude that it is much less significant to God than it is to most of us. Yet a lot of young Christians—especially boys—would put masturbation as the most significant battle line in their attempt to live as Christians. God does not, apparently, consider it even worth mentioning. So tell him not to let guilt over this issue drive him away from God.

"Understand the real problems." Guilt, addiction, hidden fears, and destructive myths are the true problems. Masturbation will not cause blindness, weakness, or mental retardation, and it won't cause a guy to run out of sperm, making him unable to father a child in the future. The best way to avoid problems with masturbation is for him to open up and discuss this issue with a trusted adult—preferably his father.

"Avoid the danger zones." Masturbation can be harmful and should be avoided if it's done . . .

- while fantasizing about an immoral relationship (see Matthew 5:27–28).
- with pornography or any other "unclean picture" set before his eyes.
- to the point of becoming an uncontrollable habit. What's uncontrollable? A general guide is several times a day every day, for months in a row. If that describes your son, he needs to talk this out with a trusted adult male. (Again, preferably his dad.)

"Strive for sexual self-control." We don't think there's anything necessarily wrong with your son thinking about sex. (It's kind of difficult for him to avoid, right?) But we do believe every male's sexual imagination has to be controlled. Why? Many guys who masturbate harbor fantasies that are plainly immoral. Again, these should have no place in a Christian's life. What's more, as we mentioned earlier in this chapter, the discipline of bringing his sex drive under control will help him to be a healthier, more fulfilled, godly person. So what do we mean by *self-control*? (1) Your son must avoid the danger zones listed above. (2) He shouldn't masturbate every day and *should* consciously strive to limit this activity as much as possible. (3) Your teen must steer clear of mental porn shows. (4) He should use the following verse as a shield—even repeat it in the face of temptation: "Flee from sexual immorality. . . . You are not your own; you were bought at a price. Therefore honor God with your body" (1 Corinthians 6:18–20).

Dating, Relating, and Waiting

Sometimes "hooking up" with the opposite sex is just about fun and recreation; not romance. My girlfriend and I really like each other, and it's come to the point where she and I want to kiss and stuff. But some of my friends say it's wrong in God's eyes to make out. To us, it's not a big deal.—Brenden, 15

All my friends are girl crazy. Not me. In fact, I'm not really interested in dating or having a girlfriend right now. Is there something wrong with me?—Scotty, 14

I'm a few months away from turning twenty, and I've never had a girlfriend, never been kissed . . . nothing! I wasn't a loser in high school either. I went to the Christmas dance with a girl, but I've never had a girlfriend. I still like this girl from high school, but I never had the guts to ask her out. Now we go to different colleges and I finally asked her to the movies last year. We had fun, and it was great—but it didn't seem as if she wanted to be asked out again. And at my school, all the girls are into drinking and stuff. YIKES! I'm going to be twenty, and I'm still alone!—Aaron, 19

Hey, my girlfriend and I like to dance, and I was wondering if grinding is wrong. I mean, it's not like a guy and a girl are really doing it when they dance.—Tyler, 16

All the other guys have started dating. They act totally cool around females. Not me. I turn into human Jell-O just talking to a girl, much less asking her out. I guess I'm afraid of saying dumb things and being rejected. Will I ever be confident around girls? What if I turn out to be a failure with the opposite sex?—Aaron, 16

Not only do most teenage guys feel some level of insecurity around girls, but many have given in to three painful myths about dating and relating:

Myth No. 1: Being "girl-less" means being less of a guy.

Myth No. 2: Rejection from the opposite sex = social suicide.

Myth No. 3: Only wimps turn to Jell-O around girls.

Dating may be a few years down the road for your son—that is, if it's an option at all. (Some families choose courtship.) Regardless, it's important that you dispel the myths and nurture confidence in your son as he relates to the opposite sex.

How Moms Can Nurture Godly Dating

Encourage him to let God define his self-worth—not the status of having someone to date. Make it clear to your son that, despite what his friends are doing, it's okay to not date. Emphasize two key points:

- It feels weird to be left out, especially when others seem comfortable with something that may make us nervous (such as dating). But we can't force something just to fit in. God wants us to trust His timing.

- Most guys *and* girls turn into "human Jell-O" around the opposite sex. Some are better at disguising their nervousness than others. The key is to relax and be yourself.

Encourage him to let God be the source of his strength—especially when he faces rejection. The number-one fear of most teenage boys is rejection from girls. Why? Regardless of race, faith, or economic background, deep in the heart of nearly every young male is the same core desire: *When I become a man, I will share my life with a very special woman.* To some degree, being rejected chips away at this dream.

While your son will never be "rejection proof"—all human relationships involve risk, right?—you can steer him to solid ground. Communicate these time-tested principles:

- "Don't set yourself up for a fall by forcing romantic expectations on every girl you meet. At this stage in your life, focus on friendships with the opposite sex."
- "Make an effort to seek God's will for your life and save yourself for His best. Ask Him to be the author of your dreams—from developing your abilities to finding the right lady."

Getting Physical: What Your Son Must Know

Help your son define his terms. When it comes to kissing, what is he talking about? Does he mean a kiss on the cheek or even a quick kiss on the lips? Or is he talking about passionate and prolonged kissing that involves petting and rubbing against each other?

We know many teens who have decided not to kiss until they're engaged; others have committed to waiting until they're at the marriage altar before they kiss. The Christian community has varied views on kissing, dating, and courtship.

We can't tell you what's right and wrong for your son, but we can tell you what we *think*. Each time he kisses a girl, he's giving a little piece of himself away. We believe a young man should be incredibly selective about whom he chooses to kiss, letting God help him with this decision. Kissing simply because it feels good isn't a good enough reason to kiss someone.

Regarding Tyler's question above about dancing and grinding, we believe that moving and rubbing and thrusting with a gal and pressing each other's body parts into each other is an act of intimacy. And the simple fact is, Tyler hasn't earned the right to be intimate with the opposite sex. When will Tyler, and your son, earn that right? As soon as he says "I do."

Express your desire for your son to live a life of purity. Explain how sexual immorality will affect his future marriage in an unhealthy way.

A Vision for Marriage

I met a girl at church camp who has all the qualities I'm looking for—including a strong faith in God. Even though we spent only a week together, I'm convinced that I've found my soul mate. But my parents believe otherwise. They say we're way too young to get serious romantically, especially to think about marriage. Our feelings are real, so what makes us too immature?—Chase, 16

I keep telling myself this: If only I can just get married, then my wife can fulfill all my sexual desires. I won't have to struggle with lust anymore. My older brother told me that lust never goes away—even for married guys. Is this true? If so, where's the hope?—Barry, 15

Perhaps you're hearing similar ideas from your son. First, applaud him if he has a mental list of what he's looking for in a girlfriend and a future wife. That's wise! Tell him you're glad that he wants to date a Christian girl.

Take him back to Bible days. Explain that if he were living about two thousand years ago, he wouldn't be too immature for marriage. Of course, he would've had a full-time job by now and may have been an apprentice for a few years prior. He'd be building his own home, or he'd be constructing an addition onto your house for him and his bride.

He would have already shouldered the responsibilities of an adult for about three years now.

Is he ready at age sixteen to support this young lady? Has he graduated high school early? What about college? Maybe he's thinking he doesn't need it. Maybe he's right. But chances are he'll never have a career without that college degree.

By asking these questions, it will help your son see that although he may not be too young to feel in love, he *is* too young to start thinking about marriage, unless he can honestly say he's already fulfilling all of the above questions you've asked.

If your teen son has thoughts of marriage with a girl, for now encourage him to date her, to spend time with her family, and to help her get to know your family. Remind him to place God at the very center of this relationship. If this is His will, He'll guide the relationship to a deeper level. If not, He'll let your son know to back off.

How Moms Can Prepare Their Sons for Marriage

Consider Barry's comments above. If your son has echoed these same thoughts, let him know that marriage is fantastic, and sex is wonderful to share with his future wife. But neither being married nor having sex regularly has the magical power to instantly change him into something he's not.

God *can* change his heart, and your son can learn to guard his heart and mind better. But marriage just means he has a partner to share his life with: the good, the bad, and the struggles. And having sex doesn't make him immune to lust.

They're enemies, remember? Why should lust quit attacking when he's found the deepest love of his life? Instead, it will just switch tactics and start trying to convince him that the other guy's woman is more attractive than his.

It's great to have high standards for your son's future wife, but where are his expectations coming from? Is he thinking about godly character or airbrushed swimsuit-model images? Sure, he wants to be physically attracted to his wife, but how would he like it if she compared him with every action-movie hero?

Tell your son this: "You can pollute or purify your mind. Your future wife will thank you for choosing the latter. And you'll thank yourself for building habits that will carry you through the marathon of beating lust."

Bottom Line: Communication Is Key

Moms, we hope you and your husband are talking openly and honestly with your son about lust, sex, and dating. We also hope you'll remind him that God never created sex to be a start-stop-start-stop activity. He created it to start and go faster and get more explosive until the end.

God wants a lifetime of sexual fulfillment for your son in a marriage that He helped design. Please pray with your boy about setting specific boundaries in his dating life. Begin praying now for his future wife. Pray specifically that . . .

- God will begin molding your son now into the godly man his wife will need.
- God will protect his future wife.
- God will draw her heart intimately to Him.
- God will begin preparing her right now to be the godly woman your son will need.

Pray these things *for* your son and *with* your son.

How Moms Can Protect Their Sons' Hearts

We urge you to make a pact for purity with your son. Help him surrender his sexuality to God so that He can sanctify it and give it back to him in all its glory at the proper time.

Set aside uninterrupted time, find a private place, and make a family pact for purity. Acquire a cross necklace, a ring, or a watch beforehand and present it to him as a symbol of purity. (Even if he has already done something like this at youth group, it's more powerful if he has this experience with Mom and Dad.)

Read 2 Timothy 2:20–22.

Talk openly about sexual matters. Be willing to answer any questions your son may have. Even go one step further and share personal struggles you faced growing up.

Communicate clearly God's design for sex.

Spend some time praying for and with your teen.

Several years back, I (Michael) called a pack of teens from my church (guys who were in a discipleship group I led), then headed to a remote spot in the Rocky Mountains.

When my church group and I arrived at our destination, I shared a true story: "A friend of mine told me about a man who lost his life to AIDS a few years back. This guy had his ashes sprinkled right here. Before his death, he committed his heart to Jesus. But he also expressed some deep regrets for not being self-controlled as the Bible instructs. If he were alive today, he'd warn you to not follow the path he chose.

"Guys, you have a chance to honor God with your lives. Let's make a pact with God to live a life of purity."

Before returning home, each one of us slipped on crosses, and the guys made vows to remain pure. Then we spent time sharing our struggles, reading Scripture, and praying for each other.

I'm thrilled to report that years later, the guys are still wearing their crosses—and are committed to saving themselves for their future brides.

I urge you to make a pact for purity with your son. Help him surrender his sexuality to God so that He can sanctify it and give it back to him in all its glory.

CHAPTER 8

Keeping Him Safe in Cyberspace: *Unplugging Porn*

Judy's son, Hunter, wasn't interested in watching his favorite prime-time TV show or taking on an Xbox video-game challenge. After glancing at his watch, then muttering something about having a big test to prepare for, the sixteen-year-old excused himself from the dinner table and raced upstairs.

The proud mom smiled at her husband. "And to think—he used to grumble at the thought of doing homework," she said, happy that her grown-up son was behaving so responsibly.

Later that evening, Judy interrupted Hunter's time on the computer with a *tap, tap, tap* on his bedroom door, then a friendly reminder: "Shut down and hit the sack."

But when she poked her head into his room, she was stunned by what she saw on the computer screen. Judy turned her head quickly and pretended not to notice. Hunter, on the other hand, scrambled to maintain his cover. He switched off the monitor, flashed a phony smile, and told an outright lie: "Thanks, Mom. Homework's done, and I'm heading to bed."

As Judy pulled shut Hunter's door, her heart began to race and she felt queasy deep in the pit of her stomach. *It can't be true,* she told herself. *Not my son. I must be imagining what I just saw.*

She put her hand back on the doorknob . . . then paused. *Should I confront him right now? Should I talk to my husband first? Is my son really living a double life? What on earth are we going to do?*

The sad truth is, what Hunter once used as a tool for learning had, lately, become a tool of darkness. Internet porn seemed to own him. And with each click of his mouse, the teen was being pulled deeper into an evil web.

Judy had to intervene . . . *fast.* But how?

Navigating a Nasty Online World

Does Hunter's struggle hit home? Do you suspect that your own son is compromising his faith?

The Internet is an amazing megalopolis of cybercircuitry with unparalleled benefits in communication, and currently more than 251 million North Americans are connected.[1] But before the young man in your life spends time online, be warned: He's just a click away from trouble. In addition to all the good stuff online, the Internet contains a gushing cybersewer of pornographic material that's invading Christian homes and trapping countless teenage boys.

According to Family Safe Media, 90 percent of eight- to sixteen-year-olds who use the Internet encounter porn regularly, usually while doing homework.[2] Eighty percent of online users between ages fifteen and seventeen have multiple exposures to hard-core sites.[3]

"The Internet has brought an interstate highway of pornography into every community, with exit ramps at every terminal or personal computer," says Dr. Albert Mohler, a national radio host and president of the Southern Baptist Theological Seminary. "Today's teenager is likely to know more about sex and its complexities than his father knew when he got married. Furthermore, what most generations have known only in the imagination—if at all—is now there for the viewing on Web sites, both commercial and free."[4]

What Christian Boys Are Saying

As an author, speaker, and former editor of a national magazine for Christian teen guys, I (Michael) receive hundreds of emails each month from guys I meet. Based on their letters, I'm convinced that fighting lust is one of a Christian young man's top struggles. About one-third of all the emails I receive concern problems with Internet porn.

As I read each boy's letter, I often hear the same cry for help: "I'm trapped, and there's no escape!" Many guys tell me that they feel defeated by their struggles with lust and porn, abandoned by God and ashamed of their weaknesses.

Here's a sample of what I'm hearing:

I'm a Christian, and I'm battling an addiction to Internet porn. I've told my parents about it, and they put firewalls on our computer. But in times of weakness, I find ways to get around them and access the stuff without Mom and Dad knowing. I feel terrible. What should I do?—Skylar, 16

I struggle big time with porn—and so do many guys in my youth group. I haven't told my parents because I'm too ashamed of myself. One day my dad nearly discovered my problem, but I lied to him and denied what I was doing. Will you pray for me to get enough courage to tell my parents?—Zach, 14

I don't have to go looking for porn; it seems to find me. My biggest struggle is with pop-up online announcements. Just one peek sends a spark through my body and a desire for more. This stuff is tearing my life apart. I'm to the point where I'm screaming out for help!—John, 19

What Parents Must Do

Fathers—*and mothers*—must take action. How?

First, don't be afraid to talk with your son about the dangers of pornography. Strive to foster an open dialogue in a nonthreatening atmosphere. And if you suspect that your son is viewing porn, don't come across like a prosecutor in a TV crime show, which will only put up walls and make him feel even more ashamed of his actions. Instead, embrace him in love, and seek to talk through his struggles. Above all, give him hope.

Second, create a "Family Purity Battle Plan" and involve your son in the process. Consider taking these steps together:

Family Purity Battle Plan

Cut off the source. Many filtering software packages will block sexually explicit material before it gets to your family's computer screen. But as sixteen-year-old Skylar admitted, they're not always 100 percent effective. Check with a product manufacturer first. Also, review the resources in "Combat Zone" below.

Set time limits. The more time he spends online, the greater the temptation to visit inappropriate sites.

Position your computer in an open place. Create a computer workstation in a common area, such as the kitchen or family room. Also, keep him off the Web when he's home alone. Secrecy only adds to the temptation.

Have your husband begin a father/son connection time. Encourage your son to be accountable to his dad on this issue. The two can pray together regularly and monitor *each other's* time online.

Study Scripture together. This is where he'll find the hope he needs in the battle. Read 2 Corinthians 10:5, Psalm 101:3, and Philippians 4:8. Print them out and place them on your monitor as a constant reminder.

Combating Porn: A Father's Struggle

The year was 1969, and thirteen-year-old Gene thought he'd struck gold. Back in the deepest, darkest corner of his father's workshop was an overstuffed cardboard box. It wasn't packed with the usual old junk. Instead, it was hiding magazines filled with incredible airbrushed fantasies.

"Oh man, I wish the guys could see this!" Gene thought. He knew about these kinds of magazines, but he never imagined finding them in his own house. "I can't believe it! They show *everything*!"

Gene was captivated by the glossy pages. Each photo fueled all kinds of weird feelings deep inside of him.

"Who would have thought that my own dad—Mr. Can't-Miss-Church-on-Sunday—actually looks at this stuff? I guess his secret's gonna be mine too."

Many years later, Gene regrets ever opening that box. He describes it as being snared in a trap—the same pornography trap that held his father in bondage.

"I knew I had to break the cycle when I discovered that my own teenage son was dabbling with Internet porn," Gene told me. "The Bible talks about the 'sins of the father' visiting future generations. That's exactly what was happening in my family.

"But I discovered that there is hope and healing through Jesus Christ," Gene continues. "The cycle can be broken—the bondage destroyed. It involves fathers leading the way for their sons. Above all, it requires honesty, repentance, and the power of the Holy Spirit."

Talking Tips

If you feel clueless about what to say to your son regarding porn, here are four talking tips that Gene recommends:

Porn devalues people. Explain that it promotes the belief that humans are not dignified beings, but instead are toys to

WHAT YOUR SON ISN'T TELLING YOU

be used for personal gratification. Women are portrayed as sexual objects and men are depicted as lust-driven machines.

Porn encourages casual sex between unmarried men and women. It also often promotes unfaithfulness between husbands and wives.

Porn is addicting. Experts agree that sexually explicit material can "hook" its users and keep them coming back for more. Medical research documents an increased flow of endorphins—hormones that create pleasure in the brain—when sexual images are viewed. Greater stimulation is needed to keep a constant flow of endorphins to the brain's pleasure centers. In other words, porn creates addicts out of its users.

Porn is off-limits to God's people. The Bible calls us to purity. In 1 Corinthians 6:18–20 we read:

> Flee from sexual immorality. All other sins a man commits are outside his body, but he who sins sexually sins against his own body. Do you not know that your body is a temple of the Holy Spirit, who is in you, whom you have received from God? You are not your own; you were bought at a price. Therefore honor God with your body.

Combat Zone

For ideas on how to guard your son's heart and mind in the cyber world, check out these Web sites.

- *Netsmartz.org*
- *SafeTeens.com*

- *CommonSenseMedia.org*
- *X3watch.com (accountability software)*
- *InternetSafety.com/safe-eyes (filtering software)*

CHAPTER 9

"Is Gay Okay?"

Why are Christians so uptight about homosexuality? It isn't considered a big deal among my friends, and I'm starting to question what I've always believed. Maybe gay really is okay.—Alex, 16

What should I say to a homosexual? A teen girl I'm friends with is a very outspoken lesbian. She knows that I'm a Christian, so she recently emailed me, asking if I thought she was going to hell. She seems pretty upset about this issue, and I have no idea what to tell her.—Nick, 15

How can someone love me and hate me at the same time? I'm a Christian teen who is living a secret life. At school and at church, everybody sees me as a nice, moral boy—the kid every mom wants her daughter to date. In reality, I'm gay. I'm sexually attracted to other guys. I crumble inside whenever my youth pastor says stuff like, "Love the sinner, but hate the sin." I don't want to be this way, yet I can't change who I am.—Chris, 17

Why am I drawn to gay porn sites? I visit these places all the time. This has been going on for about three years. I hate myself for doing it, and I manage to stop for a day or so, but then I get weak, give in, feel horrible—and I repeat the same creepy cycle. Recently, my mom caught me and cancelled our Internet service. But I'm still able to look at porn at our public library. I go there as often as I can. Once I log on and start surfing, the emptiness kicks in, and I just want to die. Am I homosexual? I've never had sex with another guy, but I can't stop looking at gay porn.—Andrew, 16

How can I overcome my struggle with homosexuality? I pray and pray that God will deliver me from my attraction to guys, but it never goes away. I try to be turned on by girls, yet my body won't do what my heart and soul knows is right.—Justin, 17

Is it possible that being homosexual is something that makes up who I am—just like the color of my hair and my gender? Everyone at church says it's wrong to be gay, and if homosexuals really want to be saved, they just need to stop being this way. But I am saved. I accepted Jesus as my Lord and Savior, and I try as hard as I can to live a life that is pleasing to Him. I'm starting to think maybe I just wasn't meant to be with girls.—Riley, 18

I love God, and I don't want to go against His will, but there's this deep struggle inside. I think I'm gay—but I want to be straight. Please don't give me the same advice I hear at church: pray harder and go get some therapy. Why can't Christians offer real solutions?—Timothy, 15

I've never thought of myself as being gay. But I absolutely love it when I see two girls kissing. It's a big turn-on, and I fantasize about it all the time. Is it wrong?—Brendan, 14

What can I do to get a homosexual memory out of my mind? When I was in the sixth grade, my friend and I started checking out what each of us had. One thing led to another and we had contact. We were so young, and it was just so stupid. A few years later, I asked him to forgive me, and he said, "Of course!" I also asked God to forgive me. Now I'm in tenth grade, and I'm still haunted by what we did. I haven't had any other sexual contacts or problems with pornography. But I just can't seem to get that memory out of my mind. Why isn't prayer working?—Luke, 16

Teen boys are asking lots of questions. But instead of engaging in healthy dialogue and finding biblical answers, too many guys are trapped behind a wall of silence. Others are caught in the crossfire of heated divisions. On one side, *tolerance* declares that you can't disagree with homosexuality . . . while on the other, *fundamentalism* says, "There's nothing we can agree about—sin is sin!"

Parents and church workers *must* talk to boys about this hot-button issue and help them clear up the confusion. Consider this about homosexuality: Television glamorizes it, celebrities embrace it, activists fight for it . . . *and teen guys struggle with it.* Yes, even Christian guys.

A Colorado kid named Brian is one of them.

I was Brian's discipleship leader at church, and I loved him like a son. We often spent time together on weekends or at Wednesday night youth group meetings. Hearing him open up about his silent battle broke my heart.

Lost and Alone: Brian's Secret Life

Brian sat across the table from me (Michael), his face strained with sadness. We had come to our favorite coffee spot to fuel up on high-octane espresso concoctions and celebrate a milestone in his life. The eighteen-year-old had been accepted by a prestigious art school in California—his boyhood dream. So why was Brian unhappy?

"I had a big fight with my dad," he explained.

"That's not good," I said, "especially with all the cool things ahead. So, what did you guys argue about?"

"Well, I've always felt that he'd accept me if I were a *real man*—a jock like my brother. But the truth is, I'm not." Brian slumped back in his seat and took a sip of his coffee. "So I told him, 'Look, I can't throw a football, so I don't measure up in your eyes.'"

"And that made him upset?" I asked.

"Not entirely. It's what I said next that really got to him."

"So what was that?"

Brian looked me in the eyes and swallowed. "It's something I haven't told anyone except my parents. Something I'm almost afraid to tell you."

This young man really had my attention now. *What is on his mind?* I had a few hunches—but hoped I was wrong.

"Go ahead. You know you can tell me anything. We're friends!"

"That's why this is so hard," Brian said. "Your friendship means so much to me. I don't want to lose it. And since my father really hates me now, I don't want to lose you too." Brian paused and took a deep breath. "See—I'm sick of being scared and hiding who I really am. It's time to be real . . . with God, with myself, and with others. So I have to tell you this. The fact is, I've known for quite a while that, well . . . *I'm gay.*"

I nodded my head calmly and took a sip of my coffee. But on the inside, it felt as if my heart were ripping apart. "Let's talk about it, Brian—as friends. That will *never* change. Tell me what's going on."

Brian shared how, since junior high, he had struggled with same-sex attraction, and how a few months earlier he'd experimented with another guy. Now he was trying to figure out where his faith fit in. "I know the Bible is totally against homosexuality, and I don't want to disappoint God. But how can I change my feelings—who I am?"

"Are you sure this is *who you are*?" I asked.

"Yep—I'm sure," he said. "I live inside this body . . . so I know what my brain is thinking."

"But everybody *feels* a lot of different things at different times in their lives," I pointed out. "So if you *feel* homosexual—and especially if you experiment with it—you can probably convince yourself that it's your identity, and therefore you can *choose* to be homosexual—right?"

"Nope," Brian said. "I've heard that line of reasoning before—usually from Christians who don't have a clue what guys like me are dealing with. This isn't just a momentary thing. So please don't tell me something like 'Just pray harder. . . . God loves the sinner but hates the sin!'"

I squinted and shook my head. "Is that what you think I'm going to say next?"

Brian cracked a smile. "No. You're different. You always listen to me, as a friend should. And that's what I need right now—a friend who will listen and not try to preach at me."

"Yes, you do need to be *heard*. And both of us should avoid worn-out lines that only shut down conversations. It's important at this moment that you connect with a trustworthy friend."

Brian nodded, and I continued. "One of those friends—the most important of all—is Jesus. I hope you're moving closer to Him, not running."

"Actually, I'm kind of running."

"But you said you want to be real—even with God. So why avoid Him?"

"I don't know," Brian said with a shrug. He fidgeted with a spoon and looked away. "Maybe it's what the Bible says about homosexuals. It's pretty harsh. Maybe it's all the stuff I hear at church. I guess I fear more rejection."

"As a believer, you're one of God's sons," I told Brian. "Our Lord cares deeply about everything you're going through. You know that. I've even heard you say this to others. So why not tell Him what you're feeling—and even share your doubts? He can handle them. Jesus loves, heals, and restores. Do you still believe this?"

Brian looked up and caught my eye again. "I guess it depends on what needs to be healed. I mean, I don't feel that homosexuality is something a person necessarily should be restored from. Can't I be His son *and gay*?"

"Ask God that question," I responded. "And think about this: Following Jesus isn't about fitting Him into our world. It's about giving ourselves completely to Him."

Our hour of coffee and conversation passed quickly, and suddenly both Brian and I had to run. Just before darting out the door, I turned to him and said, "Listen, the journey ahead is going to be hard, regardless of what you do next. But if you keep talking to Jesus, He'll show you what's real. You might not like what He says at times, but *everything* He tells you can be trusted. *God is truth.*"

Brian nodded, and we hugged good-bye.

Love: The Right Response

I wish I could tell you that Brian's life turned out "happily ever after" and that his relationship with Jesus is strong today. Sadly . . . I can't. The truth is, he's still running—and he's still searching for what's real.

If your son or another young man in your life shares Brian's secret struggle, how should you respond? Nashville-based therapist Michael Malloy suggests four things:

1. Pray. After all, God is in control. He understands what's at the root of all our struggles, and He knows how to heal a hurting heart. Ask Jesus for strength, courage, and opportunities to share the truth in love.
2. As you talk, be willing to share your own personal issues.
3. Don't condemn a homosexual for his choices. People haven't chosen to have these feelings the way you chose what to wear today. Understand that rejection is at the core of the homosexual dilemma.
4. Don't cite endless Bible verses and spend your time pointing out why homosexuality is sin, but don't go to the opposite extreme either. Show compassion and understanding, yet deal with the reality of the situation.[1]

Help Him to Know the Truth

According to Mike Haley—a nationally recognized expert on teen and homosexual issues, and a youth and gender specialist for Focus on the Family—there are three key lies about homosexuality that many Christian guys are beginning to believe.[2] Haley urges parents and youth workers to set the record straight.

The Lie: Ten percent of the population is homosexual.

Although Alfred Kinsey's research methods have been found to be pretty biased, homosexual advocates for years have quoted his 1948 book, *Sexual Behavior in the Human Male,* as the ultimate authority, proclaiming that 10 percent of the population is homosexual.

The Truth: A series of recent national studies indicates that only about 2 to 3 percent of sexually active men and 1 to 2 percent of sexually active women are currently engaging in same-gender sex.

What's the big deal about how many people are gay or straight? By saying that one out of ten people in the United States is homosexual, some gay activists are knowingly promoting a lie and declaring that homosexuality should be accepted as normal. Yet even this reasoning is faulty. For instance, 10 to 15 percent of Americans suffer from alcoholism, but we don't accept this behavior as normal or healthy.

The Lie: Homosexuals are born gay.

In 1993, the research journal *Science* published a study that ignited a "born gay" myth, claiming that science was "on the verge of proving that homosexuality is innate, genetic and therefore unchangeable."[3] The media went ballistic, heralding stories suggesting scientists had discovered a "gay gene." Only in the fine print did reporters qualify statements about this *possible* discovery, because in reality, there was *no actual* discovery.

The Truth: There is no evidence to support the claim that a person can be born homosexual. The studies just don't prove it! All the findings combined from the study of twins, gene "linkage" studies, and brain dissections cannot prove that homosexuality is genetic. Dr. Joseph Nicolosi, director of the Thomas Aquinas Psychological Clinic, comments, "Homosexuality is much more complex than mere behavior and includes many complex dimensions, including thoughts, feelings, fantasies, specific attractions and identity."[4]

Why is it so important for some homosexual activists to prove this issue? If homosexuality were genetic, people would not be able to change their orientation. If society was convinced that people are indeed *born* gay, then many would also be convinced that there is a need to protect homosexuals by the government as a designated minority class, such as African-Americans or Native Americans. This would spark states to legalize same-sex marriages, and more preschool children would be taught that having two mommies and no daddy is just another kind of love.[5]

The Lie: Homosexual relationships are no different from heterosexual ones.

Homosexual advocates want their relationships to be treated the same as heterosexual ones, enjoying legal rights to marriage and adoption. And some gay couples really *do* love each other.

The Truth: Many studies have found that the average male homosexual is far more promiscuous than the average heterosexual. Even some in the gay community admit this. Two researchers who professed to be a gay couple concluded that gay relationships between men rarely survive if they are not open to outside sexual contacts.[6]

God created the unique relationship between a man and a woman. Yet He is equally unhappy with premarital sexual relationships as He is with homosexual relationships. He intended neither. To say that homosexual relationships are the same as heterosexual ones is to make a mockery of God's divine act of Creation and His ordination of marriage (Genesis 2:19–25).

Truth and Tolerance

As Christians, we know that the sacredness of life is based on God's character—not our characteristics. We truly are not our own; we were bought with a price. Knowing this, we should not be cruel to anyone different from us, including homosexuals. We must respond to people in love, just as Christ did. Yet showing kindness, respect, and love for others doesn't mean we have to affirm all that they do.

What the Bible Says

Do not lie with a man as one lies with a woman; that is detestable. (Leviticus 18:22)

Therefore God gave them over in the sinful desires of their hearts to sexual impurity for the degrading of their bodies with one another. . . . Because of this, God gave them over to shameful lusts. Even their women exchanged natural relations for unnatural ones. In the same way the men also abandoned natural relations with women and were inflamed with lust for one another. Men committed indecent acts with other men, and received in themselves the due penalty for their perversion. (Romans 1:24, 26–27)

If we confess our sins, he is faithful and just and will forgive us our sins and purify us from all unrighteousness. (1 John 1:9)

CHAPTER 10

The Furious Five:
What Guys Need

Ask a teen guy what he needs and you'll probably get these answers:

"I need meat!"

"I need to clobber something."

"Money! I need money."

"A girlfriend."

"Huh?"

"A car."

The list above represents *felt* needs but not necessarily *real* needs. When we've been able to get teen guys to think past the surface (by bribing them with pizza and video games), they came up with needs that are real *and* felt.

Though he won't express these needs to you, here are five really important needs that your son has.

He Needs to Discover His Identity

> This whole macho thing really warps us guys. I even have a hard time setting a Christian example around my friends at school. It seems that every day I mess up. I cuss, take part in crude jokes, and even bully other kids. I really want to be a solid Christian guy, but it feels like my "wiring" is messed up. What should I do?—David, 14

It shouldn't surprise us that teen guys are trying to figure out who they are; after all, many guys in college and even in their mid-twenties are still seeking the answer to this question. But you can help your son discover his true identity early by guiding him into an intimate, growing relationship with his Creator.

Before we begin with your son, however, we actually need to start with *you.* Are you confident in who *you* are? The only way to avoid an identity crisis, and the only way to truly be confident in who God created you to be, is to live and thrive in an intimate relationship with Him.

So before we go any further, would you mind pausing right now and assessing where you stand with Jesus Christ? If your identity isn't grounded in your Maker, you could easily be headed toward an identity crisis of your own in a few years. Let's stop right now and pray about it.

Dear Jesus:

I realize you, as my Creator, know me better than anyone in the entire world. You understand my identity because you wired me uniquely in your image. I don't want to face an identity crisis in a few years; I want to be confident in who I am, in who you created me to be.

So, Jesus, I'm placing my life in your hands. I'm admitting I'm a sinner. I'm so sorry I've disobeyed you and have broken your heart. Will you forgive me? I realize that forgiveness and eternal life are gifts from you. I don't deserve these amazing gifts, but I want them. And I'm accepting them from you right now.

Thank you for wiping my slate clean. Thank you for forgiving me and granting me eternal life. Now help me to really start living for you. Show me who I am in you. Solidify my own identity, so I can help my son discover who he is in you.

Dear Jesus, I want to be confident in my identity. I realize if I'm not, my son will pick up on it. Thank you for living inside of me. Draw me ever closer to you each day of my life. In your name I pray these things. Amen.

Here's the exciting thing about having a relationship with Jesus Christ: The more you get to know Him (through reading your Bible, prayer, and spending time with Him), the more confident you'll become in who He created you to be. And who's going to be watching all this? Your son!

A confident parent is very attractive to a teen guy. *Why?* Because that's exactly what *he* wants! So determine to guide your son into intimacy with Christ. Here are a few tips:

Read and study the Bible together. The more you familiarize yourselves with God's Word, the more confident you both become. Your emotional—as well as your spiritual—strength will come from hiding His Word in your hearts.

Pray together. It is extremely powerful yet humbling to walk into the throne room of God and pour out your hearts to the

Father on each other's behalf. This will teach your son that there's nothing so big he can't pray about it, and there's nothing too small to pray about. If it concerns him, it concerns his heavenly Father. You can teach him this truth by approaching God together in prayer.

Discuss spiritual truths together. What's your theology? Is doctrine important? Why do you believe what you believe? Helping your son understand these things and teaching him how to articulate them will give him confidence when sharing his beliefs with others. Get some good apologetics books and enjoy some theological discussions together.

He Needs Friends

I battle with loneliness. In fact, I don't feel accepted at church or at school. I'm often left out of things like parties and get-togethers. I've been at my church for about four years now, and nothing has changed. Nobody ever calls me or texts me.

It really hurts me to be left out. I try to reach out to people, but they just look at me like I'm a freak. I've considered leaving my church—even my school. I've prayed, but there's no change. I really feel lonely. I wish I could learn how to connect with others.—Jeremiah, 15

Hey, I'm scared to death of rejection—even as a Christian—and I don't know how to deal with this. I'm in grade nine, and I try to stick up for God and Jesus, but the kids in my class always laugh at me. It's so hard living in a small town with one good friend to talk to. I want to stand strong for God, but I'm tired of being rejected. I really need help.—Jesse, 15

Every teen guy in the world needs to feel connected and accepted and that he matters. If Jeremiah doesn't eventually learn how to connect with people, his desperation for acceptance will become so strong that he may turn to alcohol, drugs, premarital sex—anything that will make him feel accepted by others.

Here are some things you can do to help your son:

Model good friendships in front of him. It's normal for teens to be awkward with people skills and developing friendships. Dads should model positive interaction with male friends. Moms, make sure he hears how you relate to your friends on the phone and in person.

By demonstrating good people skills, you're teaching him how to communicate with others. Engage him in some role-playing. Pretend he's someone you want to become friends with. Show him how a great conversation should happen. Often teen guys just don't know what to say and how to say it.

Make your home a friendly place. Your son may not feel as though he has any friends to invite over, but you can volunteer your home to the youth pastor. Perhaps on a Friday night or Sunday evening the youth pastor and students from the youth group could come to your house for refreshments and a movie or games. In doing this, you're helping your son reach out to his peer group. Watch how he interacts with others, and talk about it later.

Pray with your son about friends. Ask God to bring him one friend, and start praying together for that friend every day.

Help him discover Bible heroes who were often lonely. Let your son know that there are times when he *will* be alone, and that's okay. Take a couple of weeks to read and discuss together the story of Joseph (Genesis 37–47). He was certainly alone when his brothers threw him into a pit. He certainly had no friends when his brothers sold him as a slave to the Egyptians.

Imagine what it must have been like to be in a foreign culture, unable to speak or understand the language! He was taken advantage of and lied about by Potiphar's wife. He was forgotten for a long time by the "friends" he had made in prison. Yes, God was faithful to bless him, and eventually his life turned out far better than Joseph would ever have imagined.

Take a week to read and discuss together the story of Daniel (Daniel 6). Discuss what it must have felt like to be thrown into a den of lions completely alone.

Take a week to read and discuss together the story of Shadrach, Meshach, and Abednego (Daniel 3). What must it have felt like to be so persecuted? How did God deliver these young men?

Remind your son that although there will be times he'll feel rejected, alone, and unloved, he's in good company! Remind him that God will *never* leave him, and memorize this verse together: "And surely I am with you always, to the very end of the age" (Matthew 28:20).

He Needs Boundaries

I want my parents to be my parents—not my best friends. Please don't try to talk like me or dress like me or let me screw up. It's okay to set boundaries. It shows that you care about me. The best thing you can do is set the example for me.—Sean, 16

Though I doubt Sean—or any other teen guy—would admit this in front of his parents, guys really want and need boundaries. Your son's developmental years are not meant for you to be his friend. They're meant for you to guide him into healthy development mentally, physically, emotionally, and spiritually.

There *will* be a season in which you and your son can experience more of a friendship of equals, but that usually happens in his mid-twenties or thirties. Right now, your son needs to be guided. He needs Mom and Dad to step up to the plate and call the shots.

I (Susie) used to have a 160-pound Saint Bernard named Bosco. He was extremely mellow. Walking him around the block twice a day was all the exercise he wanted or needed. The rest of the time he was perfectly content to simply eat, sleep, and be loved on by me.

He eventually passed away, and I decided to replace him with a small dog. (Though I love big dogs, I was afraid I'd always be comparing the new dog to Bosco, so I purchased something completely opposite.) I got a miniature schnauzer and named him Obie. He weighed only five pounds when I brought him home.

I bought everything he needed: a kennel, doggie blankets, toys, food, you name it. I was encouraged to crate-train Obie, so for the first few months he spent a lot of time in his kennel. After he was housebroken, and as he reached his one-year mark, I decided to start giving him a little more freedom. *After all,* I thought, *he probably doesn't even like his kennel anymore. He'd love to have the run of the house like Bosco did.*

So I began leaving him out in the house while I was gone. I soon realized that Obie truly missed his kennel. I'd leave the door open, and with the entire house to run around in, he'd go inside his kennel and curl up with a toy. I began to realize that his kennel—even though it represented boundaries and restrictions—was also a place of security for him.

Surprisingly, it works the same way with your teen son. He may scream and beg for no curfew, but deep inside he *needs* and *wants* boundaries. There's something secure about knowing that Mom and Dad are expecting him home at a specific time.

Your rules can also offer him the security of rejecting invitations he doesn't feel comfortable rejecting on his own. For example, check out what one teen guy told his mom: "I'm gonna ask you if I can go to this party, but I need you to say no so I can say you won't let me."

It's much easier to say, "I can't. My parents are too strict" instead of, "No, I don't think that's the proper environment for me, and I may be tempted to do something I'll later regret."

He Needs Help With All the Sexual Feelings He's Experiencing

I battle with lust every day, and it really makes me weary. In fact, it's so much easier to give in than to fight. Every Web site, magazine, and billboard we see features women who are either half-naked or posing in a way to get guys to lust after them and do something that we'll regret later.

Even the popular Web site MySpace has ads that say "Find single hot women in your area and maybe you can get lucky," or "Sometimes it's nice to be naughty."

How do I get around those and not lust afterward? How can I make the right decisions?—T.S., 15

Let's first begin with the importance of knowing—really knowing—if your son has a relationship with Jesus Christ.

Though being a Christian won't remove temptations, it *does* help to know that Christ can empower him to keep from yielding to temptation.

Memorize this Scripture together:

> But remember this—the wrong desires that come into your life aren't anything new and different. Many others have faced exactly the same problems before you. And no temptation is irresistible. You can trust God to keep the temptation from becoming so strong that you can't stand up against it, for he has promised this and will do what he says. He will show you how to escape temptation's power so that you can bear up patiently against it. (1 Corinthians 10:13 TLB)

Make sure your son is plugged in to a youth group and with other Christian guys. Of course, as his parent, you need to be setting the example by being plugged in to church as well.

Search yourself and your home and analyze hour habits. Are there things you're doing that could be making it tough on your son? For example, Mom, are you walking around the house in your undies? Is Dad viewing magazines, movies, or TV shows that magnify your son's struggle to remain pure?

If so, be willing to change your behavior and activity. Work hard to create a godly environment for your son to thrive in. Notice I said "work hard"? This *will* be *hard work*! It will require you to be on guard and teach your son how to be on guard.

When I (Susie) was growing up, there were two TV shows my brother and I weren't allowed to watch. When I tell you what they were, you'll laugh. Today, these shows seem completely innocent and even clean.

We weren't allowed to watch *Gilligan's Island* and *I Dream of Jeannie*, and it was all because of the way Ginger and Jeannie dressed. You'll remember they dressed scantily, and my parents didn't want us to think this was acceptable behavior. They didn't want my brother to be tempted by those images, and they didn't want me to think I could dress that way. So those shows were banned from our household.

There were many times my dad turned off the TV and said, "Let's just spend some time praying together." We called it "family altar time." We'd kneel wherever we were (me by the piano bench, my brother by the sofa, Mom by her chair, Dad by his recliner) and take turns talking to God.

This taught me that there's nothing too big and nothing too small to talk to God about. If it concerns me, it concerns Him.

You want your son to learn this same lesson. So do everything in your power to remove as much temptation from the home as possible. You want to establish your house as his safe haven. So be very discerning about movies, TV shows, magazines, and books. Also, get a filter for your computer, and don't allow your son to have a computer in his room. Place it in the kitchen or somewhere very visible so he'll be less tempted to click on sites he shouldn't be in.

Temptation is tough. We have to do everything in our power to eliminate the temptation from our home; then we can take it to God and ask Him for help.

Also, help your son develop some accountability in this area. The ideal person to help with this is his Christian father. But if he doesn't have that, ask the youth pastor at your church about the possibility of establishing a small group for teen guys to pray for one another and hold each other accountable in the area of sexual purity.

He Needs Confidence

I'm such a dork. I'm no good at sports, and kids in P.E. make fun of me. I don't feel comfortable around girls yet, and I'm only an average student. I can't play an instrument or sing, and I have no idea where I fit in. I just wanna feel good about myself, you know? Like I have something to offer.—Troy, 15

Troy isn't alone! In fact, he's expressed what thousands of teen guys feel. It's important to expose your son to as many varied activities as possible, so he *can* discover what he's good at. Excelling at something—or even being able to simply be okay at it—will give him confidence.

My (Susie's) nephew has loved the arts and drama since he was a small boy. But his parents signed him up for T-ball, soccer, and other sports simply so he'd know how to play. He also took gymnastics lessons, piano, dance, and voice. Even though sports aren't his thing, he's actually good. His parents wanted to make sure that if he went to camp during his teen years, he'd never feel isolated because he didn't know how to swim or play softball or soccer. He knows how to compete in these areas, but today in his mid-twenties, he's pursuing professional acting.

Your son may never enjoy piano, but why not expose him to it? Again, the more things he learns to do—even though he may never pursue them—the more confident he'll be, and the easier it will be for him to discover what he *is* good at.

Maybe your son is a great mechanic, but he doesn't know it yet. Perhaps he's tech savvy and could create Web sites or develop computer animated movies. Help him discover what his gifts are. Once he finds something he loves, he'll become good at it. And in the process, he'll become confident.

CHAPTER 11

Anger and Depression

His eyes were wide, his jaw was tight, his fists were clenched at both sides, and his voice cracked. It was almost that of a man, but it still rang with the high-pitched tone of a child. His words, on the other hand, could take down the strongest parent.

"I can't stand you!" fourteen-year-old Eric screamed from the top of his lungs. "You are suffocating me. You never give me freedom or trust me with anything. You never listen to my side . . . and you're always on my case. Why can't you just LEAVE ME ALONE?!"

With that final angry outburst, Eric stormed out of the kitchen, leaving his frustrated mom, Tracy, feeling devastated. Eric would be back, and more words would fly . . . along with another painful explosion. At least that had been the pattern for the past several weeks. Before that, he seemed unusually withdrawn—even down at times. Were her junior-higher's

WHAT YOUR SON ISN'T TELLING YOU

emotions normal? How could a mom allow her teen boy to treat her this way? And at what point should a parent seek professional counseling for her child?

Tracy poured a cup of coffee and took a seat at her kitchen table, her mind spinning. *I used to scream back during our arguments,* she thought. *And I'd usually ground Eric or take away privileges, but the anger seems to be mounting. Every explosion is worse than the one before. And when he's down, he goes lower than I've ever seen before. What's going on inside that heart of his? Where's that smile he used to wear all the time?*

But on this particular day, Tracy couldn't shake off her son's remarks. She worked hard at being a good parent, and she didn't want to raise a son who screamed at people when he didn't get his way. She simply could not accept his angry outbursts.

But what on earth should I do?

Tracy had to act—FAST!

Does the scene in Tracy's kitchen hit home? Are you a mom who feels at the end of your rope too? We're not surprised if you're nodding your head yes, because similar parent-teen conflicts are played out countless times a day in households coast to coast. But to echo Tracy's concern, "What's going on?"

Here's what some guys have told us. . . .

Recently I've had a growing problem with depression and anger, and I'm at my breaking point. I really don't know how to control the outbursts. I explode at something extremely small or insignificant, and I'm not sure how to handle the depression either. I've seen several counselors, yet nothing seems to happen except I get worse and worse. I have trouble getting out of bed and even wanting to do anything at all. Here's what's really scary: I discovered that some of my friends are into cutting. I always thought that it was strange, but I tried it. I now understand how people can cut themselves. Now I'm addicted to it like a drug. I want to keep doing it. I don't know what else to do.—Josh, 16

I grew up in a Christian home and was saved at a young age, but now I'm completely depressed. When I was twelve, my dad started getting violent with me. It only happened a couple of times a year, but it has left permanent scars—physically and emotionally. Up to that point, I'd been homeschooled, but I entered public school in the eighth grade. I had zero social skills and was the butt of every prank and joke. I had death threats made to me, I was robbed, and the officials did nothing about it. Grades nine through eleven got better, but I still struggled with depression, lust, and cutting. I'm now in twelfth grade, and I have solved my battles with lust, but the depression and cutting have gotten much worse. Last weekend I cut myself more times and deeper than I ever had before. I've never done drugs in my life, but just today I took three prescription narcotics. I can't find anything to fill this emptiness. I really need help—but I don't know where to turn!—Max, 18

I got a bad grade in school, so my parents took my phone away. Now I can't talk to my girlfriend, and I won't be able to see her for a while. Anger is welling up inside me, and I just want to scream! I really don't know how to control my emotions. Is this a guy thing? —Mannie, 16

I've been depressed a lot, and I know a bunch of stuff has contributed to this. My parents divorced when I was seven. My dad has never been there for me, and I haven't even talked to my mom in about two years. I've never gotten along with my older brother.

But recently my depressed mood is lingering. It usually doesn't last more than a week, but I've been feeling this way for more than a month. It's been causing a slight pain in my chest and is making my asthma worse.

Some things have changed that I'm sure have contributed to this: My little sister was put in a foster home, I'm under a lot of stress at work, my girlfriend broke up with me because she's living with another guy who's twice her age, I'm having trouble keeping up in school, and I stopped hanging out with my friends in gangs who are doing drugs, so I don't have many friends I can talk to or hang with any more. I drink quite a bit but not as much as I used to. I know alcohol is a depressant, but it seems to help me relax and feel better. I've been trying to read the whole Bible, but I haven't gotten very far. I don't know what to do about the depression.

I talked to a therapist for a while after my parents divorced, and I hated it. I don't want to do that again. I used to talk to my youth pastor about stuff, but I never told him about everything. It's hard for me to tell anyone about how I feel; that's just not how I was raised. I did tell him I drink, and he seems to pretend like I don't and it's not a problem. He did come with me to one AA meeting, but he hasn't said anything to me since. I don't know what to do! I can't stop drinking. I always feel sad and lonely. I know people who are depressed are at risk of committing suicide. I've had thoughts about it, but it's not something I'd ever do, so don't worry about that.—Jason, 17

Guys' Emotions: Some Assembly Required

As we've said throughout this book, a teen boy's emotions rise and fall like a wild ride on a roller coaster. In a given day, lots of unrelated items can push his internal anger button: parents, teachers, friends, siblings, hunger, lack of sleep. He can feel lonely if a friend moves away. He can end up depressed if he fails an exam or is rejected by a girl.

Experiencing all of these conflicting emotions is normal. When your son is angry or depressed today, when everything feels as if it's going wrong and life doesn't seem to be worth living, he needs to ride it out. It may not feel very good for him, not to mention your family, but if he can work through these feelings, he'll discover that his circumstances will change tomorrow. His world will seem much better. Happiness will return, and the anger, loneliness, or depression will disappear.

But it's not healthy if your son gets stuck in one or more of these emotions. If his anger feels extreme to you or out of control, or if he isolates himself for several days, you may need to seek the advice of a medical professional.

Anger—God's Way

Even though many Christians feel uncomfortable expressing anger, the Bible actually offers guidelines on getting angry the *right* way. It's up to you to teach your children what Scripture says, beginning with Ephesians 4:26–27. In this passage Paul says, "'In your anger, do not sin': Do not let the sun go down while you are still angry, and do not give the devil a foothold."

This passage makes it clear that anger isn't the sin. It's what that anger can *lead* to if your family doesn't head it off with God's help. Teach him a threefold strategy for dealing with anger:

Help him understand that it's okay to be angry sometimes. Point to Christ as an example. Explain to your son that several times during His ministry, Jesus became angry with the scribes and Pharisees. Why? Because they taught people to follow the wrong path to God and thus led those people straight to the gates of hell.

Teach him to be angry without sinning. While most guys know how to get angry, it's this second step they need to work on. Help your son express his anger the right way. In other words, the silent treatment and screaming matches don't accomplish anything. If something is important enough to get mad about, then it's important enough to try to work out the conflict.

Encourage your boy to . . .

- shift his focus away from the emotion and concentrate on dealing with the situation as Jesus would.
- pray before he blows his top.
- channel his anger into constructive action . . . such as finding a workable solution instead of letting angry words or actions escalate into a bigger problem.

Tell him to never let the sun go down on his anger. Encourage him to quickly settle whatever has him angry. Tell him that he should try his hardest to settle an issue before going to bed.

Remember Tracy at the beginning of this chapter? The weary mom chatted with a close friend, who just happened to be a Christian therapist, about Eric's dilemma. Here's what she learned about her son: "If your boy's angry outbursts are not satisfactorily heard and dealt with by you, his emotions could be expressed in other types of negative behavior," the therapist explained. "How? Things like poor grades, bad friends, shop-lifting, drugs, sex. It is a subconscious attempt to get back at the parents—what professionals refer to as 'passive-aggressive' behavior."

This wasn't yet the case with Tracy's son. Her boy was still blowing his top and screaming at the top of his lungs. So she decided to make an effort to really listen when Eric felt angry and to strive to help him process his emotions.

Here's what happened:

"I shut my mouth and opened my ears." One night Tracy sat at the kitchen table with her son and allowed him to express his anger—uninterrupted. In other words, she let him air his grievances. Then she asked questions calmly and allowed Eric to talk more. The more she listened, the more the angry tone decreased.

"I uncovered what was bugging him." Once she stopped focus-ing on his tone and the way he was expressing himself, she got to the source of his anger. Her goal was to hear him clearly, then work on a conflict resolution.

"I found some common ground." Once an appropriate period of active listening or shared meaning had passed (see chapter 4), Tracy and Eric came to a compromise. Then Tracy said this to Eric: "Thank you for sharing with me your anger about that situation. That means a lot to me. We won't always see eye-to-eye on things, but I always want us to listen and *hear* each other. In the future, let's strive to express our feelings more calmly."

In the weeks that followed, Eric's attitude began to change and the smile that Tracy missed finally returned.

Loneliness

Loneliness strikes at the strangest times. One minute your son is on top of the world—then, in the next second, he's plunging deep into a pit. Actually, we've all been there, so we have a pretty good understanding of the disappointment and pain we endure. And at times like this, we can't help wondering, *Where are all of my so-called friends? What could I have done to avoid this?*

If you suspect your son is dealing with loneliness, don't allow him to get bogged down by all the crazy emotions inside. Instead, help him to get some perspective, and take a moment to honestly evaluate his situation.

Encourage him to ask himself some questions:

- What's making me feel so lonely? Am I anxious about something? Is some other unresolved issue at the root of my emotions?
- Am I not enough? Can't I find wholeness in the fact that I'm God's creation? Can't I still feel secure in my identity in Christ—even if that means being alone from time to time?
- What steps am I going to take to get through this loneliness?
- Do I feel lonely, anxious, or fearful more often than most people I know? Do I need professional help to work through these emotions?

Tell him it's okay to cry. Boys don't have to be embarrassed by all those raw, uncomfortable feelings tangled up inside. Tell him this: "Turn your eyes toward heaven, and let the tears flow. Jesus understands. He'll be right there with you."

Here's a good reminder from author C.S. Lewis:

The thing is to rely only on God. The time will come when you will regard all this misery as a small price to pay for having been brought to that dependence. Meanwhile (don't I know) the trouble is that relying on God has to begin all over again every day as if nothing had yet been done.[1]

Help him connect with Christ. Communicate that falling on his knees and praying is right where he should be. Tell him that he can pour out his heart and tell Jesus everything he's feeling—*everything*! "God, I feel alone, angry, jealous, scared. I desperately need your help!"

Depression

We often misuse the term *depression*. We toss it around to describe lots of different feelings. And sometimes those feelings—hopelessness, jealousy, grief, anger, sadness, inferiority—can play a part in depression, but it doesn't mean we're actually *depressed*.

Depression is more common than you might think. It affects millions of people around the world—and depression isn't picky. It can affect your pastor, actors, musicians, teachers, you . . . or even your son. But there's more than one side to depression.

A depressed mood is different from actual depression. Being in a depressed mood is usually connected to a certain situation and won't last for a long time. For instance, if your son recently got cut from the football team, he may feel deep sadness for a few weeks, but eventually he'll get back to being himself again.

Clinical depression isn't always attached to a specific cause. It's more long-term, has a variety of symptoms, and can include certain types of depression such as *major depressive disorder, dysthymic disorder,* and *bipolar disorder.*

While we don't want this to sound like a medical textbook, we do want to give you a peek at what depression is and help you know if your son is experiencing it.

Major depressive disorder: First of all, don't be alarmed if you've felt a few of these things yourself; that doesn't mean you're depressed! But someone who's experiencing a major depressive disorder will usually have at least five of the following symptoms for more than two weeks, and it will be hard for him to continue his normal routine.

- Irritable or sad most of the day—all day long.
- No longer interested in activities he once loved.
- Weight loss (without trying to lose) or weight gain (more than five percent of body weight in one month), loss of appetite or increased appetite.
- Not being able to sleep or sleeping too much nearly every day.
- Feeling tired and worn out nearly all day every day.
- Restlessness.
- Battling with huge amounts of guilt on a daily basis.
- Feelings of worthlessness—to the point of not being able to function as he used to.
- Lack of ability to concentrate or make decisions.

Dysthymic disorder: Besides being depressed, people who experience this disorder are tough to get along with. They tend to be extremely critical and negative and have difficulty relating to others.

Those who suffer from a dysthymic disorder have usually been depressed for at least a year. Here are some of the symptoms of one who's experiencing a dysthymic disorder:

- Low energy, tired a lot.
- Can't sleep—or sleeps too much.
- Not hungry—or always hungry.
- Lousy self-esteem.
- Difficulty making decisions; hard to concentrate.
- Feeling hopeless.

Bipolar disorder: It's normal for a teenager to have mood swings. But someone who's battling a bipolar disorder will have mood swings that go way past normal. You'll see him go from being depressed and being at a point where he can't function normally to being so full of energy that he'll talk constantly, not need much sleep, and feel really good about himself. For example, he may work on a project for hours on end without sleeping or eating and still have energy for something else, but when the downside hits, he may not even get out of bed to shower or get dressed. Those extremes aren't normal.

So Now What?

If your son is truly depressed, it's not because he's wacko or a bad person. Sometimes the chemicals in our brains just get a little off balance and we simply need to see a physician who can prescribe medication to help realign those chemicals.

Depression *can* be linked to events that have happened in your son's past, and he may need to see a professional counselor. Or he may need medication *plus* counseling to get through his depression.

We sometimes have the incorrect idea that Christians shouldn't be depressed because we have a relationship with Jesus. But isn't that like saying Christians shouldn't have to go to the dentist? Or Christians shouldn't get shingles? When we have physical problems, we see a physician. Why is it so tough for us to realize that sometimes our mind, brain, and emotions need professional help as well?

We know that only a professional can truly diagnose depression, but here's a list of questions that may help you gain insight on whether your son is battling depression. If you think he would respond yes to just a couple of these questions, he's simply dealing with sadness or anger. But if you think your son would answer yes to *many* of these questions—and if he has experienced all of them close together (like in the past year)—he may be clinically depressed and need professional help.

- ☐ Has there been a death in your family during the past year?
- ☐ Has a close friend died during the past year?
- ☐ Has your pet died or been lost in the past year?
- ☐ Have you recently broken up with your girlfriend?
- ☐ Do you have a close friend who has rejected or betrayed you in the past year?
- ☐ Has one of your best friends moved away in the past year?

☐ Have your folks separated or divorced in the past couple of years?

☐ Have your folks been fighting a lot more than usual during the past year?

☐ Do you see one of your parents a lot less than you used to?

☐ Has your family gone through a financial crisis in the past year? (Has Mom or Dad lost a job and is now unemployed?)

☐ Have you moved to a new location in the past year?

☐ Have you changed schools in the past year?

☐ Do you have a family member who has experienced serious depression in the past year?

☐ Has a brother or sister left home (for college, a marriage, a job) in the past year?

☐ Does anyone in your family abuse alcohol or drugs?

☐ Do you have a family member who has been seriously injured in the past year?

☐ Have you experienced an injury or an illness in the past year that has forced you to cut back on normal activities?

☐ Do you have an ongoing illness (epilepsy, diabetes) that limits your activity with friends or is a source of arguments between you and your folks?

☐ Have you been frequently concerned about recent body changes?

☐ Have you developed physically faster or slower than most of your friends, and do they tease you about it?

☐ Do you usually maintain low self-esteem?

☐ Are you extremely critical of yourself?

- ☐ Do your folks place unreasonably high expectations on you and become upset when you don't meet those expectations?
- ☐ Do you have a family member who is very critical of you?
- ☐ Is it really tough to communicate right now with your folks? Are you yearning for a closeness that you used to enjoy with them?
- ☐ Do you have a learning disability?
- ☐ Is it hard for you to make or keep friends?
- ☐ Do you find yourself wondering obsessively if your parents really care about you?
- ☐ Are you feeling smothered by strict parents who don't allow you to express anger or share your opinions?
- ☐ Are you being emotionally or physically abused by someone close to you?
- ☐ Have you been sexually abused?
- ☐ Do other students gang up on you and give you a hard time?
- ☐ Do you feel like a failure when you do something that's less than your best—or when you make a grade that's not as high as you expected?
- ☐ Have you had a negative run-in with one of your teachers this past year?
- ☐ Has a stepparent been added to your family in the past year?
- ☐ Has your immediate family increased during the past year due to a birth, adoption, grandparent moving in, etc.?

☐ Do you have a brother or sister who has drawn your parents' attention excessively to him/her? Have your folks often made remarks such as, "If you were more like (your brother/sister) . . ."?

☐ Have you met a goal recently (graduation, honors, special recognition) that has been exciting to you, but now that you've met it, you're feeling a letdown?

If the signs are pointing to clinical depression, please don't . . .

- throw your hands in the air and give up.
- expect him to "get over it." He can't just get over it. He needs professional help.
- ignore him.
- tell him he's too difficult to understand anymore.

Please do . . .

- remind him that God wired him and knows exactly how he's feeling. Suggest that you pray *together*.
- hug him a lot.
- take him to a professional counselor and a physician.
- give him space when he needs it.
- let him know you don't understand what he's experiencing but that you're committed to seeing him through it and will find the help he needs.
- encourage him a lot (with notes, words, cards).
- keep telling him you love him.

When Should You Get Help for Your Son?

Get professional help for your son when . . .

- your son becomes extremely withdrawn and wants to be alone more than he wants to be with friends and family. Has he lost interest in school, church, and friends?
- his depression has lasted for a few weeks. Has he emotionally detached himself? Is he more argumentative than usual? Does he require a lot more sleep?
- his self-esteem has hit a new low. Is he constantly putting himself down? Is he more negative about himself than usual?

One last thing: Keep in mind that boys are like boomerangs. Despite the angry outbursts and clashes you encounter almost daily, those countless moments you've invested in your son—nurturing him, teaching him right from wrong, and preparing him for life—ultimately will pay off. He will come back to the vital lessons he learned from you. So take a deep breath and keep telling yourself, "God is faithful!"

CHAPTER 12

What He Needs From Mom

I need my mom to be a mother—not a flake. I'm sorry if I sound disrespectful, but I think her morality is slipping. (And that scares me to death!) First, she's been skipping church, saying that it's okay to not go every now and then. (It's been almost two months now.) Whenever I talk to my dad about it, he says that she needs to figure this out herself with God. If God's talking to her, I doubt she's listening. I'm not sure how to confront her on this.

Then there are other ways that she's slipping. For example, she's been watching Sex and the City daily, saying it's really about relationships. She uses the excuse that my brother, my dad, and me watch House and Scrubs, but we turn away if it gets too raunchy. (Innuendo seems to be the exception in those shows, where Sex and the City has casual sex at its core.) Anyway, I need my mom back. She's supposed to be a role model. But it's like she's gone back to her teen years.—Brent, 17

Guys need to hear specific things from their moms. Let's take a look at the top seven.

"I'll Be a Godly Role Model for You"

Brent articulated this extremely well in his letter to us. He felt as though his mom was reverting back to her teen years, and unfortunately, many moms *are* still living in that time warp. Mom, your son doesn't need a mother who's cool, with it, popular, or in the know about stuff. He simply needs a mom who's a reflection of Christ.

Will you determine to be a godly role model to your son? This is a huge commitment. (But if you're a Christian, it should be the norm.) Even though we talked earlier about establishing a relationship with Christ, let's be sure you feel grounded spiritually. This is essential in order for you to be a godly role model to your son. Take this quick quiz, and please answer the questions honestly.

True	False	I've experienced and expressed remorse for my sins. I've repented in sorrow to Christ and have sought His forgiveness.
True	False	I believe Christ has forgiven my sins. (See Romans 3:22–24.)
True	False	I have placed my faith in Christ and have given Him control of my life.
True	False	I still mess up, but when I do, I ask God to forgive me, and He does.
True	False	I understand that prayer and reading my Bible are necessary ingredients for my spiritual growth.

True   False   I have made a covenant to serve God the rest
                 of my life.

Mom, if you couldn't answer True to any of the above statements, will you take time to make it right before God *now*? If
you don't have a genuine relationship with God, you'll never
be the godly role model your son desperately needs to become
all that God dreams for him. Is there any spiritual business you
need to do with the Lord? Do it now!

It's not fair to expect spiritual aspirations of your son if
you're not being the spiritual example he needs to emulate.
The apostle Paul told the early Christians to watch his life and
learn from him.

Mom, you too can be that confident in your relationship
with Christ. You can be so in love with Jesus that you'll wisely
tell your son to watch your lifestyle and emulate what he sees.
Does that mean you're perfect? No. But you can have a perfect
heart without perfect behavior.

Let's take a peek at 1 Peter 1:15–16. "But just as he who
called you is holy, so be holy in all you do; for it is written: 'Be
holy, because I am holy.'"

We tend to think of holiness in terms of perfection and
perfection in terms of behavior. But by being "perfect," God is
calling us to become one with Him. He wants to sanctify us,
cleanse us from unrighteousness, and empower us to live the
godly life He yearns for us to live. He can perfect our hearts
as He sanctifies us completely.

Mom, have you asked the Lord to perfect your heart? To
cleanse you and release the power of His Holy Spirit within
you? When you do that, you begin to live in His lordship. When

His Holy Spirit saturates your life and consumes your being, His thoughts become your thoughts. Your deepest desire is to live in the center of His will. You fall so in love with Christ that you yearn to be in His presence 24/7.

You'll never be perfect in behavior until you get to heaven, but God can perfect your heart in such a way that you truly want His will over your own will and relinquish your rights to His authority.

Does this mean you'll never mess up? No. God won't transform your humanity until you get to heaven. While you're on earth, you're still human, and you'll still have human emotions and make mistakes. But the difference is found in your heart. Your motive, your desire, your yearning is to do the will of God. So when you *do* mess up, you simply seek your Father with genuine repentance (meaning you're not only sorry for your sin, but you're also turning away from it), and He is faithful to forgive. That's not weakness, it's spiritual growth!

And the closer you grow to Christ, the less attractive the things of the world will appear. Let your prayer be, "Dear Jesus, help me to fall in love with you more and more every single day of my life. Teach me how to truly live in your presence 24/7." When you're praying this way, you're also being a godly role model to your son. When you turn down his request to watch a specific movie, he knows that you're not going to go see it later with your husband. When you monitor what he reads and the time he spends on the computer, he knows that you're not reading trashy romance novels or entering chat rooms and flirting with men. In other words, he knows beyond doubt that you live what you say. Your words match your actions.

Your son desperately needs to see you as his godly role model. He needs to see that the blouses you wear aren't too revealing and your jeans aren't pasted on. He needs to see that you don't look longingly at a handsome man walking by. He needs to see a lifestyle of integrity through your actions, your words, and your character.

When you're accidentally given too much change at the grocery store, he needs to see you give it back. When you're stopped for exceeding the speed limit, he needs to notice that you accept responsibility instead of making excuses or being defensive. He needs to hear you ask for forgiveness. He needs to see your devoted love for God.

Will you make a commitment to be a godly role model for your son? In doing so, you're not only reflecting Christ to him, you're also demonstrating the kinds of qualities that are important to look for in his future wife.

"I Love You"

A boy desperately needs to feel loved and accepted by his mother. Dads help launch boys into manhood, but moms nurture boys into becoming great young men. How can you help your son know beyond all doubt that you love him, and that you'll love him forever?

- Refrain from being sarcastic to him.
- Never make fun of him.

- Encourage him to be his very best.
- Tell him often that you love him.
- Show him often that you love him. (When you're at home, hug him and kiss him on the cheek. Show appropriate affection.)
- Go out of your way to do special things for him (cook his favorite meal once a week, buy him a new shirt just because, etc.).
- Be his biggest cheerleader.
- Make sacrifices for him.

"I'm Here for You"

Connor realized he was in over his head when he saw a group of college guys bringing beer into his friend's apartment. Jason's parents were gone for the weekend, and though Connor's better judgment told him to stay away, he accepted Jason's invitation to the party.

Only fifteen, he hadn't started dating yet. The beer was opened and passed around. Connor managed to say no the first couple of rounds, but as time went on, the pressure mounted and he gave in.

Then the games began. Before long, spin the bottle melded into more than a game. And when Connor found himself inside a closet with a college girl who was unbuttoning his shirt, he was both excited and afraid.

After some heavy kissing, he grabbed his shirt and made an excuse to leave. The girl opened the closet door and told the group that he was a baby, a scared little virgin.

Connor left the apartment and headed down the stairs, punching the numbers on his cell phone. It was midnight. His mom answered. "Hello?"

"Spelunker," Connor said. Then he rattled off the address to Jason's apartment, hung up, and sat on the curb. His parents arrived five minutes later.

What happened?

When Connor turned thirteen, his parents took him out to dinner one night and said they would always be there for him. "Son, you know the rules we have about parties, curfews, alcohol," his dad said. "And we expect you to follow these rules."

"But we also want you to know, Connor," his mom said, "that if there's ever a time when you're somewhere you shouldn't be—"

"Maybe you're in over your head," his dad said.

"And maybe you didn't plan on the evening turning out the way it did," his mom interjected, "we want you to have a code word."

"Remember how you used to love exploring Robber's Cave when we vacationed in Oklahoma?" his dad said.

"Yeah!" Connor said. "I love that cave."

"Well, we're using the word *spelunker*," his mom said. "That's our code word."

"And, son, if you ever call us and say that word, we'll know safety is the issue and you need us to come get you immediately," his dad said.

"We're not going to yell at you for being someplace you shouldn't be, or ask questions—that will all come later . . . because you know there are always consequences for your actions," his mom explained. "But at that specific time, we're simply going to come get you and bring you home to safety. Do you understand?"

"Yeah, I guess so," Connor said. "All I have to do is say *spelunker* and you'll come get me immediately?"

"That's right."

"Cool."

"This doesn't give you permission to break any of the rules," his dad reminded him.

"But hopefully it will help you realize that we're your safety net," his mom said. "We are here for you, Connor. No matter what you do, where you go, or what choices you make, you'll always have our love, and you can always feel safe with us." Then she repeated, "Connor, we're here for you!"

"Wow," Connor said. "Thanks. That means a lot. Don't worry. I won't abuse this."

"We hope you'll never have to use this code word," his dad said. "But there may come a time when you're in trouble and you need help. We're here for you."

Can you imagine the security and confidence your son will have knowing beyond all doubt that you're there for him? You can give him that confidence by creating a special code word between you. It's for his safety.

"I'm Proud of You"

My mom is awesome. I know I'm not the best player on our junior-varsity basketball team, but she makes me feel like I am. I love it when she comes to my games. She doesn't yell or embarrass me or anything, but when we get home, she goes nuts. I'll never admit this to her, but it makes me feel like a million bucks. Like I'm gonna become a professional NBA player or something.—Aaron, 16

A boy needs to feel that his mom is proud of him. He receives validation in his masculinity from his mom. It's his dad that *teaches* and *demonstrates* masculinity to his son, but it's the mom who validates it.

- Take every opportunity you have to tell and show your son how proud you are of him.
- Praise him when he does something good—no matter how small. "Thanks for loading the dishwasher!" (He doesn't need to know right then that the glasses were loaded incorrectly.)
- Show him how to treat a woman (teach him to open your doors, pull out your chair, help you with your coat, etc.), and later express how proud you are of the gentleman he's becoming.
- Don't express in negative ways what he should have done better: "Congrats for making an A in science, but you really should have made A's in English and history too." Instead, twist it to a positive statement: "Hey! You made an A in science! Let's celebrate with brownies tonight. Way to go! You know, I'm guessing you could probably swing an A in English and history too. You're a smart guy! Let's set a goal for that, and when you reach it we'll go out for steaks."
- Let him hear you bragging about him to your friends and extended family.

- Make or buy him special cards that allow you to express how proud you are to be his mom.
- Tell him it's a privilege to have him as your son.

"I Pray for You Every Single Day"

My parents—especially my mom—are always trying to get me to tell them stuff that's going on in my life. So even though it was hard, I told my mom I like this girl and was thinking about asking her to the dance. She just kept washing dishes and told me that was nice. Why'd I even bother? I need her to know that this is huge for me! I mean, I need help. I wish she'd pray for me and take it seriously.—Lucas, 15

When your son realizes that you actually walk into the throne room of heaven and petition the King of Kings for his well-being and for His favor, he'll begin to exhibit a healthy confidence that no one can shake.

I (Susie) am fortunate to have a huge spiritual heritage. My grandparents, parents, aunts, and uncles all pray(ed) for me daily. I know that because they told me. They wanted me to know they were talking to God about me! That not only gave me confidence, but it made me want to live up to that incredible spiritual heritage.

Because of the great amount of time my relatives spent in prayer for God's hand to be on my life, I didn't even *want* to rebel. I wanted their prayers to be worth their efforts.

Several times growing up, I "caught" my mom praying and reading her Bible. Do you realize what that does for a child? It made me *know* how important her relationship with Christ was! And I learned that my own relationship with

Christ needed to take on the role of importance God desired for me to give Him.

I remember one particular night when I was home from college on Christmas break. I had the flu and was up at all hours. My most recent trip to the bathroom happened at around five-thirty or six in the morning.

As I walked down the hall, I noticed a light on in the den. When I went to turn it off, I saw my dad kneeling by the couch with his Bible. "Dad, what are you doing up so early?" I asked.

"Oh, honey, I'm praying for you. This is where I pray for you every morning," he said. I went back to bed ever so grateful for godly parents who *daily* entered the throne room of God on my behalf.

Today, as a fifty-something man, my brother still kneels each night and walks into the throne room for his family. His sons see him praying for them and know that he's taking their requests to the Father. My brother is simply emulating what he saw my mom and dad do when he was growing up. And the result is that he's now the godly leader of his own family.

Mom, isn't that what you desire for your son? That someday he'll be the godly leader of his own family? Then let him know you're praying for him every single day. It will make an incredible difference in his life!

"I Won't Give Up on You"

Okay, I blew it. I snuck outta the house and hung out with some friends. They shoplifted some small stuff and got caught. I didn't take anything, but because I was with them, I got in trouble too. Yeah, it was stupid, and I know that. But I feel like my mom's never gonna trust me again. I feel like she's so ashamed of me she doesn't even love me anymore. I'm really sorry, and I've told her that. I don't think I can handle her not loving me.—Sawyer, 16

Your son needs to know that you'll never stop believing in him, that you'll always expect the best of him, and that you'll be patient with him when he doesn't hit the mark.

Will you take a short break right now and put this book down? Grab your Bible and read the story of the prodigal son found in Luke 15:11–32.

What does this story have to say about not giving up on your son? Though the son made some huge mistakes, how did the father treat him when he returned? Did the father want the best for his son?

This father never gave up hope for his son. He knew his son's potential. Instead of focusing on his mistakes, the father chose instead to help his son reach his fullest potential. You can do that with your son as well, by letting him know you'll never give up on him.

This isn't an excuse to let him get by with sloppy behavior. Hopefully you love him too much to allow him to settle for less. Always encourage him to become all that God dreams for him. This gives you another chance to be his greatest cheerleader!

"I Will Help You Unfold the Unique Personality and Gifts You've Been Blessed With"

My mom's really smart. So I guess she thinks I should enjoy school. But I don't. I mean, I always do my homework, and I make average

grades, but I'll never be the genius she is. She makes me feel dumb.—
Grady, 17

My (Susie's) mom and dad are very detailed people. Organized. Logical. I'm not. I'm just the opposite: spontaneous, creative, it'll get done later. With Mom and Dad, everything had a place, and everything was always in its place. I lose my keys, my purse, and my passport at least once a week.

They saved. I spend.

They love quiet evenings. I want people and laughter and noise.

They both think before they speak. I speak . . . and then wonder if I should have.

They're disciplined. I'm not.

Mom worked ahead of time on things that were due; she'd do a little each day until the task was completed. I wait till the last minute and pull an all-nighter.

When they began to realize our differences, they didn't try to fit me into their personality mold. They gave me room to be myself. Mom encouraged me in sports, even though she never participated. She enjoyed hearing about my water-skiing trips with the youth group, though she was afraid of water.

She helped me join a craft club when I said I was bored and wanted to make something.

She didn't force me to cook or stay indoors. She helped me unpack the creativity that God had blessed me with. She took me to the library and introduced me to biographies of creative people. She encouraged me to write and sing and act.

She encouraged my brother to excel in basketball, though she herself never played. She never enjoyed camping, but she went anyway and made sure we had a great time in the outdoors. She was afraid of guns and wild animals, but she encouraged my brother when he wanted to learn how to hunt.

My parents gave me the freedom to develop the gifts and abilities God placed within me. Of course, I needed guidance, and they stepped in to guide me even though their interests and skills were often in other areas.

Find out what your son is interested in. This can sometimes be a process. Often a child or teen doesn't know what his gifts are, and he has to try several different things to discover his interests and his abilities.

As we've mentioned before in this book, expose your son to hundreds of suggestions: ventriloquism, riding a unicycle, making ice cream, inventing a new board game, creating a video game, launching a Web site, starting a blog, building a tree house, changing the oil in your car, training an animal, etc.

Be patient. Be willing to endure the drums, swim meets, spelling bees, saxophone—whatever it takes to help him discover the gifts and personality God has placed within him.

Why is this so important? Because God has created your son to be an individual, not a carbon copy of you. Instead of yearning for him to be more like you, celebrate the differences you share. Learn to respect and admire the funny twist he spins on a story or the attention to detail he puts into painting the mural on his bedroom wall.

As you help him unfold his unique personality, you're helping him come into himself, believe in himself, and learn how to use his gifts to glorify the Giver. Will you commit with your son to help him unfold the unique personality and gifts with which he's been blessed?

First Things First

Mom, before you actually start doing these things, please spend some time with God first. Tell Him how desperately you want to give your son these seven things you know he needs to hear from you. Acknowledge that you can't do it on your own and you need His supernatural help.

Now take a few minutes to pray through each of these seven areas. Commit all seven areas to God. After you've prayed through these areas, plan a special evening with your son. Go through each of these seven areas with him and tell him you're committed to each one. Create the special code word that he may need to use someday. Then end your time by praying with your son.

Michael's Gift of Hope

It was Christmas Eve—a joyful time, a family time. So why did I (Michael) feel so depressed? For one thing, my mom and I were alone.

I was seventeen, and my five older siblings (three brothers and two sisters) were grown up and out of the house—and unable to come home for the holidays. As for my father, he had deserted my family when I was a young boy.

The truth is, Dad was an alcoholic—and Mom would never allow alcohol in our house. So, at about the time I was learning to ride a bike, Mom was forced to take a tough-love approach: "Get help and learn to be a proper husband and a father," she had told my dad, "or follow your addiction—and lose your family. You can't have both."

My father chose his addiction. It was a decision that broke our hearts and cracked the foundation of my family. Yet in the years that followed, my mother was determined to mend some of the fractures and hold our family together. I'm happy to say she succeeded. (To this day, my brothers, sisters, and I share a deep bond that was nurtured by our mother.)

But on this particular Christmas, I didn't feel very festive. I missed the chaotic Grand Central Station atmosphere that usually filled our house.

"Yep, this is gonna be a sorry holiday," I mumbled to myself as I slouched down in a recliner and stared glumly at our Christmas tree.

Does this thing actually have branches? I wondered. Our tree was covered with so many ornaments and candy canes and strands of popcorn, it was nearly impossible to see anything that was remotely spruce-like.

I squinted, noticing a brightly colored decoration that I had made years earlier—then a couple that were created by my sisters. *Mom has saved them all,* I thought. *This tree is like a timeline of our lives.*

As I followed the "timeline," memories began to flood my mind. Mostly good ones.

My eyes focused on an oddly shaped antique bulb that was passed down from my grandmother. I couldn't help thinking about all the family traditions my mom had established. She was so proud of our heritage.

I spotted a furry, hand-stitched reindeer my mom had made—which triggered images of the long hours she worked cooking, cleaning, and doing everything possible to keep a roof over our heads.

Suddenly my thoughts were interrupted by the sweet smell of chocolate—then a warm smile.

"Let's open a gift," my mom said, handing me a cup of cocoa. "We always open one present on Christmas Eve—and this year shouldn't be any different." Before I had a chance to utter a word, she plopped a big package on my lap.

"No, Mom, let's just forget it," I protested. "Everything's all wrong this year."

Mom lifted an eyebrow. "I'd say things are pretty right," she pointed out.

I shook my head and groaned. My mom continued talking.

"Look around you," she said. "Look at where you live, and consider the food you get to eat. Some people in the world don't have any of these things. And think about the people who love you—like your brothers and sisters. They may not be here physically, but we're still a family. A strong family."

Secretly, I was tracking with everything my mom had to say, but my teenage pride wouldn't allow me to admit it. Instead, I glanced at the package on my lap and gently began tugging at the ribbon. When the last piece of wrapping paper fell to the floor, the gift was revealed.

I looked up and gasped. "Mom—you can't afford this!"

"I'm the gift-giver here, so I'll decide what I can and can't afford."

My mom had practically emptied her savings account on a present that I had talked endlessly about for years yet had always thought was out of reach. She had bought me a 35mm camera, along with various lenses.

"Every young journalist should learn to use a camera, right?" Mom asked.

I sat speechless, feeling as if I were holding not just a camera but some sort of link to my future. "This is amazing!" I said as I fiddled with the gadgets.

"There's a carrying bag in the box too," Mom said. "I figure you can take this to college with you next year."

A grin stretched across my face. "Mom, *you're* pretty amazing. You sacrifice so much for us. What would we do without you? Who would we be?"

Suddenly Christmas didn't seem so empty. And from that moment on, I began to see my mom differently. From that moment on, my world began to make a lot more sense.

That night, I unwrapped the greatest gift a teen guy could ever receive. Of course, I don't mean an expensive camera. I'm talking about the gift only a nurturing mother can give: *hope.*

Despite the hardships in our lives, my mom did everything possible to shape me into a man who was ready to face the world with confidence. She planted seeds of faith in my life and sparked in me a vision for my future. The influence my mom had on my life was *utterly irreplaceable*—and it's the same in your home.

Here are two key ways a mother influences the lives of teenage boys:

Mom Nurtures the Abilities of Her Sons

When I was seventeen, Mom bought me a camera. On other occasions, she had given me a typewriter (encouraging the writer in me) and an oil painting set (sparking the artist in me). She seemed to zero in on my talents—then looked for ways to nurture and develop them. Likewise, moms share with their husbands the important role of developing a boy's abilities. A mom is both a coach and a mentor.

A coach teaches, inspires, demands, encourages, pushes, and leads. Good coaches can create great performances in ordinary people. A mentor is a tutor and a model—a person who takes a special interest in the life of another. A mentor possesses a skill to teach and a willingness to do so.

Pause for a moment and think about your son. Who is this kid? What abilities has God given him? Now think of ways that you can nurture those talents.

Please avoid a common mistake: Keep in mind that nurturing the abilities of your son doesn't mean fitting him into *your* ideal image of who *you* think he should be. Help your son discover God's will for his life, then encourage him to strive for excellence.

Mom Plants Seeds of Faith

In 2 Timothy 1:5, Paul writes: "I have been reminded of your sincere faith, which first lived in your grandmother Lois and in your mother Eunice and, I am persuaded, now lives in you also."

Even though Timothy's mother, Eunice, was Jewish, she had married a non-Jewish man who was hostile toward the things of the Lord. Timothy's father would not even allow him to be circumcised (Acts 16:1–3). It appears that Eunice shouldered the entire responsibility of raising her son in the faith; she often thanked God for the support of her own mother, Lois. Right from childhood, she made sure that she taught her son from God's Word (2 Timothy 3:15), and Timothy ended up becoming a dedicated Jewish man.

Every godly mother is a Eunice to her sons. She sets the spiritual tone and provides the example and instruction teen guys need.

That seemingly clueless boy who leaves his dirty socks on the bathroom floor could one day change his generation for Christ. (*All because he has a God-fearing, praying mom.*) God is using you to mold your son's character. And whether or not you realize it, he is tuned in to what you're teaching.

CHAPTER 13

Father Hunger and Guy Time

"Rough water ahead—paddle left!" Jeffery shouts to his fifteen-year-old son, Jonathan.

"No, Dad, let's go left, so paddle right."

"Son, listen to me," Jeffery says sternly. "There are big rocks and strong rapids on the left. We need to veer right. Quickly!"

Jonathan points downstream. "But do you see that?" he asks. "There's junk in the water. Maybe it's a fallen tree or something."

"We'll take our chances," Jeffery responds, digging his paddle into the water and stroking even harder. "We'll flip if we hit the rapids."

"But, Dad—"

"Don't argue with me. Paddle left. NOW!"

Suddenly—THUMP! BUMP!

The canoe strikes a mound of twisted branches clogging a narrow portion of Colorado's Gunnison River. The vessel begins to rock violently, but it doesn't tip over.

Seconds later the water is calm again.

Jonathan turns around and grins at his father. "Okay, you were right—*this time!*"

Jeffery high-fives his son, then slumps back in the canoe. "I think we're getting the hang of this adventure thing. Now if we can just tackle life!"

Safe Passage: Navigating the Teen Years

Guiding a teenage boy through adolescence is often like a wild ride over torrential rapids. And the key to his safe passage depends on the support and training he receives from moms . . . *and dads!*

A few summers ago, Jeffery, Jonathan, and a dozen other father-son pairs faced the rapids head on—and came away stronger. They joined me (Michael) on a four-day canoe adventure through western Colorado's canyon country. Our mission: Bond in the backcountry and nurture healthy father-son connections.

It takes cooperation and communication to keep a canoe stable, making these the perfect vessels for bringing families together for shared adventure and deepened relationships. But the greatest ministry happened back on shore when the men and boys gathered around a campfire, discussing the lessons they learned on the river. Inevitably, they "pulled off their masks" and shared what was inside.

"I'm so proud of you, Jonathan, for trusting me today," Jeffery told his son one night. "We were a solid team, which is how God wants us to be."

Jonathan smiled and put his arm around his father. "I thought you were a hero out there," he said. "That's how I see you, even though I never actually say it."

Fourteen-year-old Joel opened up for the first time about his fears since becoming a teen. "The other kids are brutal," he said.

"I didn't realize that life has been so tough for you," his dad responded, "but we're going to work through these troubles— together."

As I sat back and watched the generations bond, I quickly realized that (1) teen boys are as diverse as the world in which they live, and (2) navigating them successfully into manhood requires the consistent time, attention, and understanding of an available father.

A Role Only a Dad Can Fill

My dad is definitely my hero. He makes family time a priority. When he's home, it's like my mom and sister and I have his full attention. I'd say the most important message I hear from him is, "I love you." And the most important action I see is him getting into my life and spending time with me.—Sean, 18

Dad isn't perfect, but at least he makes an effort to be my role model. Is he my hero? Sometimes. At least I hear two messages from him pretty consistently: He tells me daily that he loves me and that he'll always be here for me.—Jonathan, 15

I don't even feel as if I know my dad. It's like there's this giant invisible wall between us. We're both so busy we rarely do things together. Is he my hero? No way.—Luis, 16

These are real voices from real boys—each with different perspectives on their father-son connections. Which quote best represents your son? Is Dad the hero he needs?

Regardless of their backgrounds or cultural differences, all teen guys are at a stage in their lives when they yearn for the affirmation and companionship of an adult male mentor (preferably their own fathers). According to Donald M. Joy, PhD, professor of Human Development at Asbury Theological Seminary, there are two critical periods of a boy's life when he needs a man's influence. From birth to six years of age a boy "rehearses" his masculinity from his father. Then during the teen years a boy is released from the nest by his dad. A father instinctively teaches his adolescent son how to launch confidently into manhood.

"But if a boy is abandoned by his father," Dr. Joy writes, "or if Dad is too busy, gone too much, is an alcoholic or is otherwise caught up in his own problems or his career, the boy can suffer seriously."[1]

Be a Home-Front Hero

Sure, your son probably looks up to athletes, musicians, and actors, but nobody can replace his father. Get deep into your boy's heart. An available, loving father guides, nurtures, and strengthens his son in three key ways:

- He offers a positive model of manhood.
- He builds his son's self-concept.
- He shapes a young man's values.

But what should you do if, as Luis pointed out above, there's an "invisible wall" between a father and a son? Here's how Dad can rekindle the connection—and even become the *home-front hero*.

Know the keys to his heart. Guys need to hear important messages from their dads: "I love you," "I'm proud of you," "I trust you," "I'm here for you." *Home-front heroes use these keys to connect.*

Be willing to say you're sorry. Face it: No parent is perfect. When fathers blow it with their sons—breaking promises or flying off the handle—they should be willing to admit it and even ask for forgiveness. *Home-front heroes understand that humility and openness are the foundation for a healthy relationship between a parent and a child.*

Pray daily for your son. Fathers should not only pray for their sons, but pray *with* them as well. While this sounds like a no-brainer, it's amazing how many families neglect this important activity. *Home-front heroes pray regularly for the young men in their care.*

Nurture his faith. Show your son that while he can't outsmart or outmuscle the flesh or the devil on his own, victory over daily struggles against sin exists. The Lord has armed every Christian with spiritual weapons packed with "divine power": (1) the Sword of the Spirit—the Holy Bible, and (2) prayer. Colossians 3:16 tells Christians to "let the word of Christ dwell in you richly," and Philippians 4:7 promises that "the peace of

God . . . will guard your hearts and your minds in Christ Jesus." Help your son grasp that merely hanging out at church and "doing his Christian duty" doesn't cut it. *Home-front heroes teach boys to know Jesus personally.*

Give fatherhood "a face." Most Americans believe they know what good fathering looks like. Several years ago, a TV poll conducted by ABC News asked viewers to rank the best media fathers. Americans who responded selected Bill Cosby's affable Cliff Huxtable as their ideal dad. A distant second place went to Jimmy Stewart (George Bailey in *It's a Wonderful Life*), and third place went to Hugh Beaumont (Ward Cleaver on *Leave It to Beaver*).[2]

That same ABC News poll discovered that balancing work and family demands was a father's biggest challenge. Not surprisingly, 60 percent of those polled said spending time with their children was the best thing they could do for their children.

Dads simply have to put down the newspaper, set aside their work, and carve out a healthy block of father-son time. At first your son may treat you like an outcast and gravitate toward his friends. He may act as if he prefers his marathon phone conversation to quality time with Dad.

Yet now more than ever your teen needs your guidance. Spend time alone with your son at least once a week. Shoot hoops together, take walks, grab a Coke—anything! But make sure you give your son ample opportunity to talk. And remember this: Teens want and need your attention but often just don't know how to ask for it.

Take note of what Sean, from the email above, said: "Dad makes family time a priority. When he's home, it's like my mom and sister and I have his full attention." *Home-front heroes make daily communication a priority.*

Give him the applause he needs. A smoke-filled stage in Kansas City explodes with pyrotechnics and computerized laser lights. A teen drama troupe decked out in flashy costumes jumps, rolls, tumbles, and dances onto the scene. Their high-action performance bursts with a frenzied mix of dramatic elements: ballet, music, and mime.

Backstage, the adrenaline is running just as high in the star performer. Sixteen-year-old Terry, who plays the lead role, limbers up his legs prior to making his entrance. The second he gets his cue, Terry steps under a spotlight and launches into character. He's met with thundering applause.

Right in the front row one of the young man's biggest fans—his proud father—is clapping and cheering the loudest.

"Break a leg!" Terry's dad shouts with a wink. He bows his head and whispers a prayer: "Lord, please give my son the courage and confidence to do well. And let him perform for your glory, not his. Above all, let Terry know how valued he is to you—and to us. Amen." *Home-front heroes encourage and build the self-confidence of the young men in their care.*

Raising a High-Value Kid

Whether your son steals the show on stage or scores a touchdown on the gridiron, a father must communicate the truth about his son's identity: He's a high-value kid.

"Like wet clay, teens are still malleable," says pastor Paul W. Swets in his book *The Art of Talking With Your Teenager.* "They are breaking out of their childhood molds and entering a new and qualitatively different realm of thinking, feeling and acting.

It is confusing but exciting. Teenagers need their parents' knowledge and support to survive."[3]

The key to launching a teenage boy successfully into manhood depends on the applause he receives from his dad. Are you building confidence in your son's life? Are you affirming the unique individual God has created him to be?

Applaud your "star-in-the-making." Try this:

Tune in to his feelings. Try to look at events at home or at school from your son's point of view. If your teen senses that you don't really understand or care, he will stop listening to you. But when it's clear that you're doing your best to understand, the chances are much greater that your son will tune in to you. Despite how it feels at times, teen guys really do want their parents to talk to them; they want to believe they have someone who will listen, who will understand, who will make them feel better.

Give him your blessing. Jesus was in a river when He received this blessing: "This is my Son, whom I love; with him I am well pleased" (Matthew 3:17). If the Son of God received a verbal stamp of approval from His Father, then we can all benefit from affirmation. "I'm proud of you. I love you. I enjoy watching God shape you into a man." There's special power when those words come from the mouths of fathers, and even the toughest teen guys admit they long to hear approval from their moms and dads.

Teen Guys Need Other Guys

We've explored the crucial role dads play in launching boys into manhood. Now let's turn our attention to another important issue: Your son's need for *guy time.*

And to get a better handle on this, let's catch up with a group of male backpackers, somewhere in California's Yosemite National Park. There's nothing quite like a campfire to get guys talking. Staring into glowing embers beneath an infinite canopy of stars has a way of moving a young man's soul beyond the mundane and into the ultimate issues of life. Let's listen in on this campfire conversation about life, struggles, and the rough road to manhood. . . .

"I'm sick of all the pressure," admits seventeen-year-old Will. "At school I have to put on this stupid tough-guy act around my friends and live up to their idea of what's cool and manly. I wish I could just be myself."

Sam, age sixteen, nods his head in agreement. "People don't understand the garbage we have to put up with. If guys show any kind of weakness, we're treated like outcasts."

It's day five of a weeklong backpacking trip I (Michael) am leading. The guys in my group are opening up to each other. As our campfire conversation heats up, the masks come off and the young men begin to share their deepest fears and struggles.

"I'm with Will—I'm sick of constantly putting on an act," says eighteen-year-old David. "If you don't look and act cool, guys—even Christian ones—treat each other like dirt. But secretly, we're all scared inside. I want to be different! I want what we have right here: respect."

During our backpacking adventure, I was given an honest look at the emotional and relational struggles that haunt so many guys today. I'm convinced that a young man's world is characterized by loneliness and peer fear, one in which measuring up as a man means conforming to a cruel Guy Code: always being a tough guy, never showing weakness, and never expressing true feelings. I quickly discovered that too many young men feel the constant pressure to prove themselves in classrooms, on playing fields, and especially among their friends.

Yet the guys I met voiced their desire for change.

They hungered for family support and connection—and longed to be accepted by their peers. In the words of David, "I want respect."

What steps can you take to nurture meaningful connections with friends and family, strengthen your son's confidence, and help your son begin living like the real man he was created to be?

Here are three ideas the guys suggested:

Get Connected

"Guys need other guys," Will says. "We need a band of brothers—trustworthy men who will let us unload our secrets without feeling judged. That's what I had in Yosemite, and that's what I'm finding at home."

What you can do: Help your son build a shame-free zone where he can feel free to be real—to laugh, cry, and share everything inside. In addition, help him establish "Sacred Talking Places": one-on-one times with men and other boys (shooting hoops or grabbing a Coke together), Bible studies and discipleship groups with trusted pastors.

Make Peace With Your Earthly Dad

"There are certain things I need to hear from my father: 'I love you.' 'I'm proud of you.' 'I believe in you,'" Sam says. "But since he died a few years back, I've found an adult male friend—actually, my pastor—who speaks these words into my life. But if my dad were alive, I'd do everything possible to have a good relationship with him."

What you can do: Fathers play an obvious role in helping young guys grow into men. Whether your relationship is smooth or strained, be proactive and reach out to your boy. Let him know what he means to you, and tell your son what you need from him.

But for sons whose fathers aren't around, moms can follow Sam's suggestion and find a substitute dad. Above all, remember this: God is a boy's model of a father. He is a young man's ultimate Father and wants to love him in a way he has never experienced. He will help a boy with all the battles he faces. He will show him what authentic manhood is all about.

Find a Male Mentor

"In addition to my dad, I hang out with a man who has all the qualities I want: courage, honor, integrity, and a *Braveheart* approach to faith," seventeen-year-old David says. "He lives for the things of God like a warrior in battle. He is the kind of man I want to be."

What you can do: Just before the apostle Paul died, he wrote Timothy these words: "And the things you have heard me say . . . entrust to reliable men who will also be qualified to teach others" (2 Timothy 2:2). The Christian life is meant to be a transformation from being a Timothy to being a Paul. Help your son find trustworthy mentors—in addition to you—who can teach and guide him into healthy manhood. He shouldn't slash his way through life's problems by himself. (And neither should you, Dad.) There are many godly men around who'll gladly help the two of you cut the trail.

CHAPTER 14

Wired for Risks?

You already know that teen guys are growing up in a culture awash with materialism, illicit sexuality, violence, drinking, drugs, depression, and despair. Every day, they're bombarded with mixed messages that leave them feeling confused and overwhelmed.

Case in point: Eighteen-year-old Chris was tempted to use drugs by the most unlikely source—one of his own teachers. During his last semester at a public school in northern California, the Christian teen joined one of his art classes on an unofficial field trip to a major graphic design firm in San José. Many of the students drove their own cars, while Chris and four other students piled into the back of their teacher's pickup truck.

It was an exciting trip—his new friends and he were laughing and telling stories in the back of the truck. Suddenly their teacher slid open the cab window and handed back some sort of pipe with something burning in it. The odor was sweet and weird, and Chris wasn't sure what it was. His teacher exclaimed, "This will make the trip go by faster!"

One of his fellow students looked at the pipe with a puzzled expression, then said, "Pot?! Our teacher's doin' drugs?"

Without hesitation, he then handed the pipe to Chris. The teen winced and passed it to the next student. "No thanks," Chris said. "I don't do drugs."

The pipe made its way around the entire group without anyone taking a hit. One of the girls handed it back to their teacher.

Slightly confused and perhaps a little bit high, the instructor stuck his head through the window and scowled. "What's the matter with you?" he grumbled. "You're high school students! Don't any of you know how to party?"

Today, Chris is thankful that he didn't cave in and end up as a bad witness. Yet he has Christian friends who aren't as smart. Many have compromised their faith with all kinds of crazy choices and risky behaviors.

Let's take a look at some of the temptations that Chris and his friends must sort through.

Gambling

The guys and I play some card games and put money on the line—just to make it more exciting. I admit, it's a fun way to pocket a little money. (I usually win!) What's the harm in it? It's technically gambling, but nobody gets hurt. None of us are addicted, and we're not doing a road trip to Vegas.—Manuel, 17

This addictive activity usually begins with betting on sports games. Once your son starts winning money, he gets a rush that he wants again and again, and the addiction deepens as he puts more and more money down on other activities.

Many parents tend to think of gambling in terms of horse races and other very public activities. But boys can gamble away their entire college savings without even leaving their rooms because of easy access to the Internet. (Another great reason to keep the computer in the family room or kitchen so you can easily see what your son is accessing.)

Sadly, many families have realized the problem too late—after their credit cards were maxed out by a son addicted to gambling. Our teens are receiving mixed messages from the media. The movies and TV shows portray gambling as fun. Many are glued to poker shows and watch professional gambling for hours on end. We see governors on TV encouraging their citizens to bet and telling them how it will help the economy! But talk to any parents of a teen who has battled this addiction, and they'll tell you how destructive gambling really is.

How can you know if your son is addicted to gambling? Here are a few questions to consider:

- Is he preoccupied with gambling? (Is he consistently thinking of ways to get money to gamble with? Does he relive his past gambling experiences? Is he handicapping or planning his next gambling venture?)
- Does he have financial problems?
- Does he need to gamble with larger amounts of money to achieve the desired excitement?

- Does he display a lack of focus?
- Has he repeated unsuccessful efforts to control, cut back, or stop gambling?
- Does he gamble as a way to escape problems?
- Does he participate in secretive behavior?

What Should You Do?

Directly confront your son. Ask him point-blank if he's been involved or knows anyone who has been involved with gambling. We suggest professional Christian counseling.

Choking

I watched some friends play the choking game at a party. It looked really stupid—and it's not something I'll try. But the person who they did it to acted sort of drunk and said it felt really cool. That's why my friends do it. They want a buzz.—Charlie, 14

This is also known as "the blackout game" and the "fainting game." How is it played? By intentionally strangling yourself or someone else with hands or a noose to briefly experience a euphoric state. Teens describe a "cool and dreamy" feeling. The catch is to stop before it's too late. Unfortunately, for too many teens, death is the result. Nooses are made of T-shirts, bungee cords, scarves, belts, and dog leashes.

It's an inexpensive high. Many teens allow their friends to choke them at parties. Because the choking causes a lack of oxygen to the brain, they hope to get a temporary buzz. Unfortunately, many sites on the Internet have persuaded teens to try the game and have promised it will give "the best feeling ever." More guys participate in this game than girls.

How can you know if your son is experimenting with this? Here are a few warning signs:

- He talks about the game.
- You find belts or scarves tied to doorknobs or other furniture, or on the floor with a large knot.
- He has things in his room that seem unusual, such as dog leashes when you don't have a dog, bungee cords, or choke collars.
- He's groggy or tired after coming out of his room with friends.
- You see marks around his neck.
- He has headaches, a raspy throat, or bloodshot eyes.

What Should You Do?

As with teen gambling, directly confront your son. Ask him point-blank if he's been involved or knows anyone who has been involved with this game. We suggest professional Christian counseling.

Sexting

I'm not sure what I was thinking or why I did it, but let me tell you about a stupid choice I made recently. I took nude pics of myself on my cell phone, and I asked my girlfriend (ex-girlfriend now) if she wanted me to show them to her at church. I feel really ashamed of myself, because now I can't imagine myself ever in a million years even considering wanting to do this. But I was actually going to before—and I'm a Christian. Is this blasphemous? I'm sure God wouldn't want me to show myself to someone while I'm at church. Thankfully, it never happened. She didn't make it the week I went, but I was still going to do it if she showed up, which, in my opinion, is just as bad as if I'd done it. I've prayed for God's forgiveness many times since, and I feel absolutely terrible about it. It makes me sick to my stomach just thinking about it. And now I'm scared. Am I going to hell for this?—Rich, 16

Mix a teen guy's sexual drive with technology and you've got a phenomenon that the media has called "sexting." It's defined as *texting sexually explicit language, or sending semi-nude or nude images or videos by cell phone.* One in five teens has tried it, according to the National Campaign to Prevent Teen and Unplanned Pregnancy, including kids as young as thirteen. Some teens even shoot videos of themselves engaging in sexual activity. Then they send them to their peers via cell phone. And like Rich in the email above, churched kids aren't immune to this risky activity.

What's more, many guys receive these kinds of messages from girls. For some—even if they aren't sexting—they get caught up in it by being the unwitting recipient of an illicit text. Why are our teenage sons—and daughters—engaging in an activity that's probably unthinkable to most Christian parents?

Michael Malloy, a Nashville therapist and an expert on male sexuality, explains that many guys could be doing it for a thrill or as a way to take a risk with their friends. "It reminds me of streaking in the seventies," Michael says. "I don't think a parent who catches her son in this activity should fear that he is necessarily perverted. Yet the parent must take it seriously—and put a stop to it."[1]

Teen guys who take part in this activity may be creating and distributing child pornography without even realizing it! Sexters could be in violation of state and federal child pornography and exploitation laws, including the manufacture, distribution, and possession of child pornography, or exploitation of a minor.

"This kind of risky behavior also has a way of coming back to bite the person engaging in it," Michael says. "It can be emotionally scarring for everyone involved, it can cause shame in the one doing it, and it could end up closing doors in the young man's future—especially with colleges and employers."

What Should You Do?

Check out what's on his cell phone, then sit him down and explain the facts:

- Sexting is a criminal offense.
- If a teen guy is convicted of this crime, he may face time behind bars and become legally required to register as a sex offender.
- The images he sends to a peer can be forwarded to other cell phones, causing embarrassment and humiliation.
- It takes only one person to place a sexually explicit photo on the Web. Once online, that image can end up on anyone's computer—and anywhere around the world.
- Sexting teens leave themselves open to child predators.

- This activity is sinful and is off-limits to Christians. "But among you there must not be even a hint of sexual immorality, or of any kind of impurity, or of greed, because these are improper for God's holy people" (Ephesians 5:3).

Smoking

> I started smoking before I became a committed Christian, and now I've found it incredibly hard to stop. In all honesty, though, I really enjoy it. I know it's unhealthy, but is it okay for Christians to smoke?— Owen, 18

The American Lung Association estimates that every day, six thousand children under eighteen will take their first puff of a cigarette. Of those six thousand, about two thousand will go on to be regular smokers. The fact that teen smoking rates are consistently increasing is disturbing. About 90 percent of adult smokers started smoking before age twenty-one.[2]

One huge problem with smoking is that nicotine is considered the main entrance drug into other substance abuse problems. So why do it? Teen guys often like to act as if they're dangerous (sort of the James Dean persona that America fell in love with years ago). The "bad boy" image is often alluring to a guy. And by smoking he can act on those feelings. Because it's forbidden, it becomes something more teen guys desire. The problem is that when they take that first puff, they can become addicted.

Some guys smoke because they feel it makes them appear older and wiser. Others do it simply to be accepted or to look cool. At most schools, the smokers huddle together in designated areas that become their hangout—their place to belong. They become a "family" to each other. Many guys like the appeal this gives.

Many people enjoy the buzz cigarettes give them. Nicotine acts as a stimulant to the mind, body, and spirit. When the body becomes accustomed to nicotine, it then requires more and more to help the body function normally. This level of dependence is an addiction.

If you suspect your son may be hiding a smoking habit, here are some common characteristics to watch for:

- They often do not perform well in school.
- They feel like they're not a part of the school.
- They become isolated from other students.
- They can't perform as well in sports.
- They have little hope of going to college.
- They are reported to school officials for skipping classes.
- They start using other illegal substances.
- They experience pressure from home and school and use tobacco as a form of relief.

What Should You Do?

The most effective way to prevent self-destructive behavior such as smoking is to lead by example. Are you a good role model, or is your motto "Do as I say, not as I do"? If you abuse tobacco, stop smoking. (Chances are greater that your son will emulate your behavior.)

Medical professionals agree that going cold turkey is the best way to quit. Help your son throw away his cigarettes and substitute smoking with a positive activity—such as exercise or a hobby. (We suggest that you consult a medical professional for further advice.)

Finally, tell your son to lean on his faith as the temptation heats up. Remind him of the truth: If Christ can break the chains of death in his life, He can certainly deliver him from a habit like smoking. Tell him to cling to the hope that "if the Son sets you free, you will be free indeed" (John 8:36).

Drugs

> Where I live a lot of teens smoke pot. I've tried it and—I won't lie—I liked it. Is it really wrong for Christians to do this? Didn't God say in Genesis to live off the seeds of the earth?—Sam, 15

When it comes to drug abuse, Christian boys are often just as confused—not to mention curious—as the rest of the world. In fact, researchers at the University of Colorado surveyed more than fourteen thousand junior high and high school teens throughout the United States and made an alarming discovery: Problems with drugs aren't just outside the church.

For example, when asked if they'd ever tried marijuana, 47 percent of unchurched young people answered yes compared with 38 percent of churched youth. As for alcohol use, 88 percent of unchurched teens reported drinking beer regularly as compared to 80 percent of churched kids.

And guess who is at the greatest risk? That's right—teenage boys. Despite their religious upbringing, Christian young men who are experimenting with drugs just don't comprehend how destructive casual use can be:

- They've broken the barrier of using illegal drugs and have set themselves up for a progression toward harder, more destructive drugs.

- They've committed an act that they will keep secret from their parents and other family members—which should be a red flag that something's wrong.

- They've compromised their values and have crippled their walk with God.

What Should You Do?

Give him the facts. "I'll try it just once—it can't hurt and I won't turn into a druggie." This is the lie of the century. Help your son to understand that drugs kill. Tell him this: "A high may feel good for a little while, but the drug is poisoning your body. Take in too much of it—or keep using it—and your body breaks down and dies."

Encourage your son to never get started. The best defense against drugs is to avoid them. Stress that he should never give in—even once.

Give a biblical perspective. Galatians 5:19–21 reads, "The acts of the sinful nature are obvious: sexual immorality, impurity and debauchery; idolatry and witchcraft; hatred, discord, jealousy, fits of rage, selfish ambition, dissensions, factions and envy; drunkenness, orgies, and the like. I warn you, as I did before, that those who live like this will not inherit the kingdom of God." The word *witchcraft* is also translated *sorcery* and refers to the use of drugs. And in numerous other passages, the Bible refers to drunkenness as a sin. (See Deuteronomy 21:20–21, Amos 6:1, and 1 Corinthians 6:9–10.)

Make a pact with God. Help your son understand that the Holy Spirit gives us the wisdom to make good decisions, along with the strength to carry them out. The fact is, we serve a God with guts—a God who is strong and courageous. Pray with your teen and, together, make a pact with God to never allow illegal drugs to enter the Lord's temple—your bodies!

Drinking

> Several months ago, I tried alcohol for the first time with a couple of friends. Since then, I've been tempted to drink again. What does the Bible say about alcohol?—Darren, 16

What Should You Do?

As a parent, you have the greatest influence on your son's life. We urge you to talk to him about the dangers of drinking. Dispel the myths, and point him to the truth. Don't make the mistake of thinking *Not my son; not our church.*

Sit down with your son and talk it out. Communicate this:

1. Drunkenness is completely off limits (see Ephesians 5:18).
2. Adults are permitted to drink a little wine for health reasons (see 1 Timothy 5:23). Yet in Numbers 6:3 God instructed those who wanted to make a special vow to "abstain from wine and other fermented drink."

3. Romans 14:14–21 tells us to avoid doing anything that might cause another person to stumble. So if you openly kick back with a beer, you're telling others that it's okay to drink. But your attitude shouldn't be "Hey this doesn't hurt me, so what's the big deal?" You need to ask "How will this affect my friends?"

4. First Corinthians 6:12 says, "'Everything is permissible for me'—but not everything is beneficial. 'Everything is permissible for me'—but I will not be mastered by anything."

In other words, it's not a question of "Can I drink?" It's an issue of "Should I?" Those who are wise don't try to see how close they can get to the edge without sinning. Rather, they tell themselves, "If I never take the very first drink, then I don't have to worry about ever getting drunk or hurting myself and others."

Having said all this, remind him of what the Bible says regarding three other simple matters:

- **Lying to authorities.** Is drinking with your friends something you have to hide from authorities in your life? (Exodus 20:6)

- **Disobeying parents.** If you're not yet twenty-one, have your parents given you their blessing regarding the illegal use of alcohol? (Ephesians 6:1–3)

- **Disobeying the civil laws.** If you are under the legal drinking age and still choose to drink, then you are breaking the law. (Check out Romans 13:1–7 for more on this subject.)

How Can Parents Help Prevent Self-Destructive Behavior?

Realize that the pressure to conform is a battle your son faces every day.

Know who your son's friends are and what they do for fun. Encourage him to participate in school and youth group activities. A strong self-esteem and busy schedule will go a long way in preventing him from falling into the trap of self-destructive behavior.

CHAPTER 15

Lost in Space:
If a Boy Rejects Christianity

It's tough for guys to get fired up for God, because churches and schools sometimes overlook us. Girls have more retreats, books, magazines, and stuff to help them grow. Guys are left on their own. And to be honest, I think I have a "dead, boring religion," and I don't know how to let Him transform that.—Kyle, 15

We just found out my stepson thinks he's gay but at the same time is a Christian. He's posted his opinions on his MySpace page and has been challenged by his friends that he can't be gay and a Christian. We need help. He's insistent that it's possible to be both.—Jeannie

I've tried to be a Christian, but I just can't hack it. Besides, I want to have fun. I can always come back to God when I'm old and ready to settle down.—Evan, 16

Mark Twain once told parents that when their child turned thirteen they should put him in a barrel, close the lid, and feed him through a hole in the side. When he turned sixteen, Twain suggested parents close the hole! Of course, Mark Twain was a humorist, and we laugh about his advice. But underneath the laughter, we know that the teen years are often filled with difficulty. And it's even tougher when you discover that your son has rejected your values and your faith.

Let's face it: Sometimes guys who are brought up in a Christian home still reject Christianity. Listen in on Marcia's story.

My husband, Jim, and I were Christians when we got married and were excited to create a godly environment for our children. We were very involved in church, and our three children were involved as well.

Our son, Adam, has ADHD, and it's tough for him to sit still during things like youth group, Bible study, or Sunday school lessons. This has made it difficult for him to make good friends. Others often just don't want to be around him.

We continued to encourage him, and he was a good boy— just easily distracted because of the ADHD. (Yes, we put him on medication, but that's not always the answer because of the side effects.) Though Adam never had many friends at church, he still enjoyed going and was involved in everything that was offered.

Jim and I went on a couple of international missions trips, and we took Adam with us. He thrived. He loved ministering to the children, and his tender heart was definitely evident.

After his first year of college, he fell in with the wrong crowd. Because he's never been a leader, Adam will follow just about anyone who will accept him. These guys were smoking pot and drinking, and Adam picked up their habits. He completely quit going to church and no longer showed interest in spiritual things.

He became withdrawn and either stayed out way past his curfew or retreated to his room. We were in the midst of getting him counseling when we got a call from the police station. He'd been arrested for breaking and entering and had stolen some stereo equipment.

Our hearts were broken. He seemed repentant, but we thought it was best to have him spend the night in jail. We wanted him to realize the seriousness of what he'd done.

He got involved in church again, but later picked up his habits of lying and going back to drugs. As his court appearance neared, we discovered a place called Teen Challenge. It's a Christian residence program that works directly with the courts in helping young people get off of drugs. The court agreed to allow Adam to spend a year and a half there instead of in jail.

He's been there just under a year now, and he's thriving! He's reading his Bible and truly growing spiritually. (Of course, it helps that chapel and the classes are mandatory, but he's finally serious about his faith and becoming all that God wants him to be.)

I'm glad we never gave up on him. He has a tremendous amount of potential. My advice to parents who are going through what we did: When your son turns away from the Lord, do whatever it takes to get him back. We couldn't stand the thought of Adam spending eternity in hell. Though it was hard to check him in to Teen Challenge, we knew we were doing the right thing. Do we miss him? Absolutely! But he's getting exactly what he needs.

It's truly God working in Adam's heart. When he calls and can't wait to share a Scripture, or tell us about an answer to prayer, we rejoice with him in the faithfulness of our Father.

Don't give up! And again, be willing to do whatever it takes to steer your son away from hell.

The Blame Game

As a parent, will you own the fact that you're responsible before God to provide the training and instruction that will guide your son in His way? The Scriptures warn us that it's possible for us to exasperate our children (Ephesians 6:4) and to embitter them so they become discouraged (Colossians 3:21).

When your son rebels and walks away from Christianity, it's appropriate to evaluate the impact your parenting style has had on his life.

Please don't misunderstand. We're *not* saying that your son's rebellion is solely the consequence of parental mismanagement. If you believed that, you'd also have to believe that all human behavior is caused by external influences. We know that's not true. Behavior may be influenced by genetic and environmental factors, not to mention human will and choice! If your son rejects Christianity, it's a choice he has made on his own.

But many parents still blame themselves if a son turns from God. Please don't do that. There may have been some things you could have done differently, but your son is still responsible for his own choices and making his own decisions.

After praying about it, if you feel you need to seek your son's forgiveness for anything, the Lord will give you the strength to do that. Restoration often comes in humbling ourselves to seek forgiveness.

I (Susie) grew up in a home where my parents taught my brother and me to apologize by asking "Will you forgive me?"

instead of saying "I'm sorry." I'm glad they taught me that lesson because, as an adult, there are times I have to ask others to forgive me, and it's much easier because I've been doing it for a lifetime!

Think about it: If you're genuinely apologetic about something, show it by your actions and your words. Oftentimes "I'm sorry" simply isn't enough. "Sorry about that" seems so casual, flippant.

Sorry about what? Sorry you got caught? Sorry the other person interpreted you incorrectly? Sorry what you did was considered wrong?

But when you say "Will you forgive me?" you're approaching someone in humility and sincerely expressing your sorrow.

Have you been able to seek your son's forgiveness for mistakes you've made from time to time?

Take this quick quiz to help align where you are in the seeking forgiveness department.

1. When I'm wrong,

    a. I'm the first to admit it.

    b. it takes a lot of talking to convince me.

    c. I rarely admit it.

    d. I tend to place the blame on someone else.

2. When someone apologizes to me,

    a. it increases my respect for him/her.

    b. I view it as a weakness.

    c. I tend to think *It's about time!*

    d. I'm very uncomfortable.

3. I know someone is sincere when apologizing
    a. when his/her actions aren't repeated.
    b. only if he/she cries.
    c. when he/she uses fancy words.
    d. by the tone of the voice.

4. When I need to apologize,
    a. I do so sincerely and willingly.
    b. the person I've wronged usually has to hint or come right out and ask for an apology.
    c. I try to make light of it, joke about it, and hope the need for an apology will simply go away.
    d. I struggle greatly.

5. When someone asks me for forgiveness,
    a. I know he/she is sincerely repentant.
    b. I think he/she must have blown it really big!
    c. I assume he/she is being overly dramatic.
    d. I grant it.

When we repent of our sins and ask Christ to forgive us, we're not simply saying, "Sorry about that. Sorry my sins nailed you to the cross. Sorry I broke your heart."

In the Greek language—the language in which the New Testament was originally written—*repent* means *to turn completely away from.*

What we're really saying when we seek God's forgiveness is, "Oh, dear Jesus! I'm so sorry I've sinned against you and have broken your heart. I'm so sorry I've been disobedient. Will you forgive me? I'm turning the opposite direction right now. With your help, I'm going to build accountability and boundaries in my life that will help me to never go down that path again."

That's true repentance.

That's the heart cry of someone who's genuinely seeking forgiveness.

When you apologize to someone—or seek forgiveness from him—hopefully you're not simply spouting words, but you're *turning away from* and *forsaking* the wrong you did.

That's an apology!

Mom . . . Dad . . . will you ask the Lord right now to bring to your mind anything in your life for which you need to seek forgiveness from Him and from your son?

What to Do

Let's get a stronger grip on some specifics you can do when your son rejects Christianity.

Love him unconditionally. Just as God never stops loving your son, will you do the same? Even though he has rejected all that you hold dear, continue to reach out to him. Keep telling him you love him. Let him know that you pray for him every single day. But remember, the love that you're striving for is also a love that guides and disciplines. Proverbs 13:24 says, "He who spares the rod hates his son, but he who loves him is careful to discipline him." Unconditional love isn't fluff. It's strong.

Agree to disagree. The easy thing to do is to simply stop talking about your faith. Please resist that temptation! Continue to share with your son, and keep listening to his side. It's okay to agree to disagree.

Give him clear expectations. As long as he continues to live in your home, expect him to respect and abide by your house rules. This includes curfew, paying for gas, chores, school attendance, personal conduct, clothing choices, etc.

Exert tough love when necessary. Lots of things your son takes for granted are actually privileges: having a cell phone, watching TV, using the car. You may have to remove some of these privileges for a while if he's breaking your house rules.

Don't give up. I heard about one teen guy who hated attending church but agreed to read a chapter of the Bible with his dad several times a week. By his senior year, they had read through the entire New Testament together. God's Word had begun to take root in his heart.

God won't hold you responsible for all of your son's actions. But He will hold you accountable for the way you relate to him as a parent: Love him unconditionally, but don't compromise your commitment to his responsible maturity.

Conclusion
Lead, Guide . . . PRAY!

I (Michael) stared up in disbelief at my destination—a ledge forty feet above me. I felt completely unprepared for the task at hand. *This is insane!* I told myself. *I can't climb this! The wall seems too flat and way too steep.*

I was leading a Christian family camp near Moab, Utah. Today's challenge: Scale a sandstone wall in a section of the desert called Wall Street!

Sensing my doubt, our professional guide patted me on the back. "You're ready—I promise," he said with a smile. "We've covered the basics together. Now think through each step—and have faith. The rope will protect you."

Just as I mustered up the tiniest ounce of courage, reality hit.

Todd, an eighteen-year-old who was climbing ahead of me on a more difficult part of the wall, suddenly lost his grip and began to swing helplessly across the rock. He scraped up his arms and legs. It made my legs weak just to watch. But then I remembered the guide's advice: "The rope will protect you."

It really works! I told myself. *Todd won't fall!*

The strong nylon line that was attached to Todd's safety harness literally saved the guy's life. In fact, Todd eventually regained control—as well as his confidence—and even made it to the ledge near the top of the canyon wall.

"I was learning fairly quickly, then I slipped," he told me later. "My head was pounding, and I felt as if there was nothing to hold on to. I guess I took on too steep of a climb for the first time. My lesson: Listen to my instructor, plan ahead, and don't tackle too much too soon."

Powerful lessons for rock climbing—and life!

It was hard watching Todd slide down the rock face. Adrenaline pulsed through every vein in my body. (I can only imagine how *he* felt!) But as this young man struggled to regain control and get back on course, he wasn't alone. A number of parents began to pray for him:

"Lord, protect Todd."

"Father, give him strength right now."

"Jesus, help him to find a way out of this jam."

"O God in heaven, enable Todd to make it to the top of the ledge."

Later, when he had gotten through the ordeal, I overheard a conversation he had with another teen: "I was scared, but I know the prayers of others really helped. It's really cool knowing that the adults on this trip care enough to pray for me."

Prayer is powerful. God works through it and changes lives. He will do the same for your son. But do you regularly pray for your son? Do you pray *with* him?

Before you put down this book, we have one more challenge for you: Make prayer a priority in your home. Consider this prayer of hope, faith, and healing for your family. We've also included Gen. Douglas MacArthur's famous prayer for his son. It's our hope that you pray these, or something like them, every day.

A Prayer for Your Family

O Lord God, I ask that you make our home a place of
    love and peace and light—
    where security is found,
    where trust is taught,
    where forgiveness is modeled,
    where faith is lived.

O Lord God, draw my son close to you. Protect him in
    your arms and let him sense your power today, the
    holy, eternal power that can set him free—
    free from the bondage of sin,
    free to live life as a gift of grace,
    free to dream, free to take risks, free to fail,
    free to live in faith and in hope and in love.

O Lord God, let your truth be the anchor of my fam-
    ily. Restore, repair, renew . . . and heal our lives,
    heal brokenness,
    heal rejection,
    heal hostility,
    heal fear.

O Lord God, how we need your hope. I commit my
    family to you. Let us honor you in our home.
    Amen.

A Prayer for His Son
by Gen. Douglas MacArthur

Build me a son, O Lord, who will be strong enough to know
when he is weak, and brave enough to face himself
when he is afraid; one who will be proud and unbending
in honest defeat, and humble and gentle in victory.

Build me a son whose wishbone will not be where his back-
bone should be; a son who will know Thee and that to
know himself is the foundation stone of knowledge.

Lead him, I pray, not in the path of ease and comfort, but
under the stress and spur of difficulties and challenge.
Here let him learn to stand up in the storm; here let
him learn compassion for those who fail.

Build me a son whose heart will be clean, whose goal will
be high; a son who will master himself before he seeks
to master other men; one who will learn to laugh, yet
never forget how to weep; one who will reach into the
future, yet never forget the past.

And after all these things are his, add, I pray, enough of a
sense of humor so that he may always be serious, yet
never take himself too seriously.

Give him humility, so that he may always remember the
simplicity of greatness, the open mind of true wisdom,
the meekness of true strength.

Then I, his father, will dare to whisper, "I have not lived in
vain." Amen.[1]

Notes

Chapter 1: How a Boy's World Looks and Feels

1. Gary and Angela Hunt, *Surviving the Tweenage Years* (San Bernardino, CA: Here's Life Publishers, 1988), 12.

2. Nancy Gibbs, "What Does It Mean to Be 13?" *Time*, July 31, 2005, *www.time.com/time/magazine/article/0,9171,1088701,00.html*.

3. Hunt, *Surviving the Tweenage Years*.

4. Bill Beausay, *Teenage Boys!* (Colorado Springs: WaterBrook, 1998), 132.

5. Donald M. Joy, *Sex, Strength and the Secrets of Becoming a Man* (Ventura, CA: Regal Books, 1990), 83.

Chapter 2: Breaking the Code of Cruelty

1. Tom Neven, "Teenage Torture," *Breakaway*, October 2002, 12.

Chapter 4: Teen Guy Battlegrounds

1. Michael Ross, *BOOM: A Guy's Guide to Growing Up* (Wheaton, IL: Tyndale, 2003). Interview with Lt. Col. David Grossman conducted by Bob Smithouser.

2. Diane Levin, *Remote Control Childhood?* (Washington, D.C.: National Association for the Education of Young Children, 1999).

Chapter 6: Helping Him Unmask His "True Self"

1. Dr. James Dobson, *Bringing Up Boys* (Wheaton, IL: Tyndale House Publishers, 2001), 4.

Chapter 7: Lust, Sex, and Dating

1. Henry T. Blackaby and Richard Blackaby, *Experiencing God Day by Day: A Devotional* (Nashville: Broadman & Holman Publishers, 1998), 242.

2. Bob Smithouser, "High Voltage," *Breakaway*, January 2000, 32.

Chapter 8: Keeping Him Safe in Cyberspace: Unplugging Porn

1. InternetWorld Stats, June 30, 2009, *www.internetworldstats.com /stats2.htm*.

2. Family Safe Media, "Pornography Statistics," *www.familysafe media.com/pornography_statistics.html*.

3. Ibid.

4. Dr. Albert Mohler, adapted from "The Seduction of Pornography and the Integrity of Christian Marriage," an address Dr. Mohler gave to a group of men at Boyce College.

Chapter 9: "Is Gay Okay?"

1. Michael Malloy, interview by Michael Ross, June 15, 2009.

2. Interview with Mike Haley and Jeremy V. Jones, November 2007. Portions adapted from Mike Haley and Jeremy V. Jones, "Cleaning Up the Confusion," *Breakaway*, March 2008, 29–30.

3. Jeffrey Satinover, MD, "Is There a 'Gay Gene'?" National Association of Research and Therapy of Homosexuals (NARTH) Fact Sheet, March 1999.

4. John Paulk, "Homosexuality: Not a case of genetic conditioning," *The Oregon Citizen*, January 1997, 1–2.

5. Larry Burtoft, PhD, *Setting the Record Straight: What Research Really Says About the Social Consequences of Homosexuality* (Colorado Springs: Focus on the Family, 1994).

6. Andrew Sullivan, *Virtually Normal: An Argument About Homosexuality* (New York: Vintage Books, 1995).

Chapter 11: Anger and Depression

1. C.S. Lewis, *Letters* (London: Bles, 1966), 220.

Chapter 13: Father Hunger and Guy Time

1. Donald M. Joy, *Sex, Strength and the Secrets of Becoming a Man* (Ventura, CA: Regal Books, 1990), 32

2. "Our Father's Day Poll Results," ABC News, June 22, 1998.

3. Paul W. Swets, *The Art of Talking With Your Teenager* (Holbrook, MA: Adams Publishing, 1995), 16.

Chapter 14: Wired for Risks?

1. Interview with Michael Malloy, June 2009.

2. American Lung Association, *www.lungusa.org*.

Conclusion: Lead, Guide . . . PRAY!

1. Gen. Douglas MacArthur, "A Prayer for His Son," May 12, 2005, *http://differencemakers.blogspot.com/2005/05/prayer-for-his-son-by -gen-douglas.html.*

Michael Ross is a veteran youth communicator who has authored numerous books for young people, including the Gold Medallion winner *BOOM: A Guy's Guide to Growing Up* and a bestselling devotional, *Faith That Breathes*. Michael and his family live in Lincoln, Nebraska.

Susie Shellenberger has written 57 books and is a fulltime speaker living in Bethany, Oklahoma. She speaks 43 weeks/weekends every year and recently received her doctor of divinity degree from Southern Nazarene University. Susie was the founding editor of Focus on the Family's *Brio* magazine. She has two mini-Schnauzers, Obie and Amos, and loves bright colors!

You May Also Enjoy . . .

Even the strongest mother-daughter relationships have secrets. Your teen or preteen girl is at the age when she needs you the most, yet all too often she closes herself off. Don't give her the opportunity to look for answers or comfort elsewhere. Here is a guide to the things she won't tell you about her world, mind, and heart—and what she really needs from you.

What Your Daughter Isn't Telling You
by Susie Shellenberger and Kathy Gowler